1

RESEARCH AS INQUIRY

Framing Information Literacy:

Teaching Grounded in Theory, Pedagogy, and Practice

Edited by Mary K. Oberlies and Janna Mattson

Association of College and Research Libraries
A division of the American Library Association
Chicago, Illinois 2018

The paper used in this publication meets the minimum requirements of American National Standard for Information Sciences–Permanence of Paper for Printed Library Materials, ANSI Z39.48-1992. ∞

Volume 1: Research as Inquiry
Volume 2: Information has Value
Volume 3: Searching as Strategic Exploration
Volume 4: Information Creation as a Process
Volume 5: Scholarship as Conversation
Volume 6: Authority is Constructed and Contextual

Library of Congress Cataloging-in-Publication Data

Names: Mattson, Janna L., editor. | Oberlies, Mary K., editor.
Title: Framing information literacy : teaching grounded in theory, pedagogy, and practice / edited by Janna L. Mattson and Mary K. Oberlies.
Description: Chicago : Association of College and Research Libraries, a division of the American Library Association, 2018. | Series: ACRL publications in librarianship ; no. 73 | Includes bibliographical references and index.
Identifiers: LCCN 2018011080 (print) | LCCN 2018037718 (ebook) | ISBN 9780838989388 (pdf) | ISBN 9780838989371 (set : pbk.)
Subjects: LCSH: Information literacy--Study and teaching (Higher) | Academic libraries--Relations with faculty and curriculum.
Classification: LCC ZA3075 (ebook) | LCC ZA3075 .F73 2018 (print) | DDC 028.7071/1--dc23
LC record available at https://lccn.loc.gov/2018011080

Printed in the United States of America.

22 21 20 19 18 5 4 3 2 1

Table of Contents

Social Science

Science and Engineering

Acknowledgements

We acknowledge George Mason University Libraries for the research leave granted to us to support this project. Janna would also like to thank her colleagues at Gateway Library for shouldering extra responsibilities while she focused on this book. In particular, she would like to thank Patricia West, Head of Gateway Library, who has created a supportive and collegial environment where projects like these become not only possibilities but realities. Thank you, Patricia, for your kindness, mentoring, and support. Mary would also like to thank Helen McManus and Beth Roszkowski for their support on this project, and being willing to serve as sounding boards as we worked through the design and organization of the book.

Thank you also to Erin Nevius from ACRL Press, who facilitated our book project with patience and enthusiasm. Hannah Rempel from Oregon State University served as our outside peer reviewer and we are so grateful to her for helping us shape this book.

We express much gratitude to the contributing authors of this book who collaborated with us and supported each other through peer review and multiple rounds of editing to create this work. In particular, we are so grateful to Jolanda-Pieta van Arnhem and Jannette L. Finch of the College of Charleston, who wrote six chapters of this book outlining their innovative for credit information literacy course that incorporates all six ACRL Information Literacy Frames. We have librarians and teaching faculty from more than forty higher education institutions across the United States represented in this book. Their chapters represent small slices of their hard work and dedication to teaching information literacy in an increasingly complex information ecosystem.

Introduction

Mary K. Oberlies, MA, MAIS
Undergraduate Engagement Librarian
University of Oregon

Janna Mattson, MLS
Instructional & Social Sciences Librarian
George Mason University

Within the library world, how to conduct information literacy (IL)—the best methods, activities, and practices—is something many instruction librarians grapple with, often feeling like if we view just one more webinar or go to one more boot camp, it will help us really understand what to do when we get up in front of a class. Many of us struggle with knowing whether we are achieving our instructional goals and transferring our knowledge. Instruction librarians are a vocal bunch within library literature and professional development—just ask anyone reviewing conference proposals or conducting research—seeking to share the knowledge we have gained with others to inform practice.

In 2014, we began exploring problem-based learning (PBL) within the social sciences, a project that led to us to presenting a poster at the 2014 American Library Association (ALA) Annual Conference and being invited to speak to ANSS. We were surprised by the amount of interest in this project. PBL is not new, its foundation dating back to the 1960s in the medical curriculum at McMaster's University.[1] But the interest in the project made us wonder about the experiences, knowledge, and teaching skills of other instruction librarians—how they partner with faculty, how they incorporate active learning, and how they feel about their instruction. We sent out a survey in fall 2015 asking these questions and received 156 responses—certainly not a large pool—but we noticed similarities in the responses. The instruction librarians who participated in our survey experienced similar frustrations and concerns about how to develop learning outcomes and activities, being overwhelmed with instructional jargon, having a lack of confidence in teaching due to a lack of training or subject expertise, and how to overcome student and faculty apathy toward information literacy instruction.

After reviewing the curriculum of ALA-accredited library programs, we found correlations as to why instruction librarians might experience this dissonance. As of November 2015, only one program required a course on instruction, five programs did not offer any courses on instruction, and the remaining fifty-four programs offered on average a range of one to three courses.[2] Among us, we only had one instruction class in our library science curriculum, though we have since addressed this deficit through independent research and formal education. How can librarians be prepared to teach when not provided with the basic skills and theoretical underpinnings of teaching and learning? From our findings, an idea was born to pull together a collection of lesson plans grounded in theory and the ACRL *Framework for Information Literacy for Higher Education* that relayed the experiences of the librarian creator, with the intention to shift this paradigm and empower teacher librarians.

Goals of *Framing Information Literacy*

Our first goal is to address the teaching anxiety and insecurity librarians often experience by offering narratives with the lesson plans that provide insight into the work involved in developing a polished lesson plan. Many chapter authors offer past teaching failures that have helped them to arrive at their lesson plans. It is not often that we get an inside look at the work that goes into successful IL teaching, and it is encouraging to be reminded that teaching is an iterative process for everyone.

The second goal is to begin filling the teaching and learning knowledge gap for librarians in the context of IL. We have captured the knowledge and practice of fifty-eight teacher librarians and five teaching faculty from forty-one institutions for others to incorporate and build upon. Each lesson plan is grounded in a learning theory, pedagogical approach, or instructional strategy that is either well established or emerging in the field of education.

Our final goal is to capture how teacher librarians use the ACRL *Framework for Information Literacy for Higher Education* in conjunction with educational theory and pedagogy to help readers form their own approaches to teaching IL. While chapters are focused on one particular frame, some authors point out that their lessons touch on more than one. Other authors use theory and pedagogy to fill in the gaps the Framework generously provides teacher librarians.

How to Use *Framing Information Literacy*

Recognizing that the needs of teacher librarians vary from day to day, we have organized this book set so it can be used multiple ways. The chapters provide approachable explanations of the ACRL Frames, various learning theory, pedagogy, and instructional strategies, and how they are used to inform the development of information literacy lesson plans and learning activities. Each volume includes one frame, and readers are encouraged to navigate them by subject/discipline, special population, or by learning theory, pedagogy, or instructional strategy. For readers new to the field of education, we offer these definitions:

1. Learning theory: the way in which a learner learns best, based on assessment and/or observation. Not one learning theory is preferred over another; rather, learning theories provide understanding as to why desired learning outcomes are best met when learning environments are situated in a way and for a group of learners.
2. Pedagogy: the practical application of teaching. Some chapter authors use the term andragogy, which is the teaching of adults, as pedagogy is sometimes used to refer to the teaching of children. For clarity, we use the term pedagogy in this book without using an age distinction.
3. Instructional strategy: the tool or method used to facilitate learning

In each volume, chapters are grouped by broad disciplinary focus (social sciences, arts and humanities, science and engineering, and multidisciplinary), making it easy to skip around to locate needs-specific lessons.

There is a standard structure to each chapter. The heading of each chapter contains information about the special population(s) the lesson considers (student-athletes, undergraduates, etc.), and the learning theory, pedagogy, or instructional strategy guiding the creation of the lesson as well as which frame concept is addressed. Each chapter starts with a discussion about how the author(s) created the lesson, any partnerships they nurtured, and an explanation of the frame and methodology and how it relates to the development of the lesson. In addition to the theoretical facets of the lesson, chapters also provide information about technology needs, pre-instruction work, learning outcomes, essential and optional learning activities, and how the lesson can be modified to accommodate different classroom setups and time frames. Chapters conclude with an assessment piece. Lesson planning and teaching are creative acts, so while the editors strived for each lesson plan to follow a consistent template, there is some variance in their presentation as everyone approaches instructional design differently. While the format varies, the same core elements are present in each chapter, and the editors hope by seeing this variance, novice teacher librarians can feel free to adopt a style comfortable to them.

As each volume contains chapters about a specific frame, readers might notice they are arranged in a different order than what appears within the *Framework for Information Literacy for Higher Education.* Each volume contains an anchor chapter written by Jannette L. Finch and Jolanda-Pieta Van Arnhem representing a single lesson from their for-credit online information literacy course. To help readers follow this scaffolded series, the volumes are arranged in the order the authors follow in their course design. This variance in order is representative of the fluidity the Framework offers, freeing librarians to identify the most appropriate learning goals for students, rather than being confined to teach to a hierarchical skill set.

Just Start Somewhere

We encourage readers to start in a place of comfort—perhaps a designated subject area. We know teacher librarians who are novices or want to change teaching methods need encouragement and collaboration, and we offer that in this book. We encourage readers to start at a place of curiosity. Many librarians we have met while writing these volumes work have wanted to try a certain pedagogy but were unsure how to begin because they had no background in education. Learning theory, pedagogy, and instructional strategies are for everyone. If something does not work for you, the reader, try something else: "Not all students learn in the same way and not all teaching techniques appeal equally to all students. To keep students interested and involved, teachers cannot rely on a single method of instruction but should instead vary the ways in which they introduce new concepts and skills."[3] Finally, we encourage readers to start in a place of need, perhaps because of an administrative mandate to teach to the Framework, begin a formal assessment program, or incorporate active learning. This work provides practical information about all three. We hope our readers will begin to see the connections between the various disciplines represented in these volumes, the various approaches to teaching, and finally the *Framework for Information Literacy in Higher Education*. So, pick a discipline, a theory, pedagogy, or instructional strategy, or one frame—just start somewhere.

Notes

1. Shelagh A. Gallagher, "Problem-Based Learning: Where Did It Come From, What Does It Do, and Where Is It Going?," *Journal for the Education of the Gifted* 20, no. 4 (1997): 332, doi:10.1177/016235329702000402.
2. There are some outlier programs like the University of Missouri-Columbia (ten courses) and Long Island University (five courses) that offered more options on instruction and assessment; however, 50 percent (twenty-seven out of fifty-four) of these programs only offer one course on instruction.
3. Marta Bladek and Karen Okamoto, "What's Theory Got to Do with It? Applying Educational Theory and Research to Revamp Freshman Library Workshops," *College & Undergraduate Libraries* 21, no. 1 (January 2014): 24–25, doi:10.1080/10691316.2014.877730.

Bibliography

Bladek, Marta, and Karen Okamoto. "What's Theory Got to Do with It? Applying Educational Theory and Research to Revamp Freshman Library Workshops." *College & Undergraduate Libraries* 21, no. 1 (January 2014): 19–36. doi:10.1080/10691316.2014.877730.

Gallagher, Shelagh A. "Problem-Based Learning: Where Did It Come From, What Does It Do, and Where Is It Going?" *Journal for the Education of the Gifted* 20, no. 4 (1997): 332–62. doi:10.1177/016235329702000402.

1

RESEARCH AS INQUIRY

Research is iterative and depends upon asking increasingly complex or new questions whose answers in turn develop additional questions or lines of inquiry in any field.

CHAPTER 1

Using Student Curiosity to Generate Compelling Research Questions

(Lesson 1 of 6)

Jannette L. Finch, MLIS
Librarian III
College of Charleston

Jolanda-Pieta van Arnhem, MFA, MLIS
Scholars Studio Librarian
College of Charleston

ACRL Information Literacy Frame: Research as Inquiry
Discipline: Multidisciplinary
Subject: Information Literacy
Learning Theory: Constructivism
Pedagogy: Metaliteracy
Special Populations: Online Learning; Undergraduate Students

The authors worked together to develop a one-credit information literacy course offered synchronously online beginning in 2009. This is the first of six chapters detailing how the authors implemented scaffolded learning assignments while incorporating developments in the field of information literacy. These developments include ACRL's 2015 adoption of the Framework of Information Literacy in Higher Education,[1] the availability of an open-source textbook, *The Information Literacy User's Guide*,[2] the recognition of a Community of Inquiry that informs online teaching and learning,[3] and a shift in pedagogical style in higher education from lecture-based to facilitator of learning experiences.

As these changes in information literacy took root, the authors visualized structuring the online class to develop the metaliterate learner through scaffolded assignments aligned with the six frames, the units of study suggested by the content of *The Information Literacy User's Guide,* and student learning outcomes.

A visual representation of this alignment, emphasizing the six frames, is seen in figure 1.1.

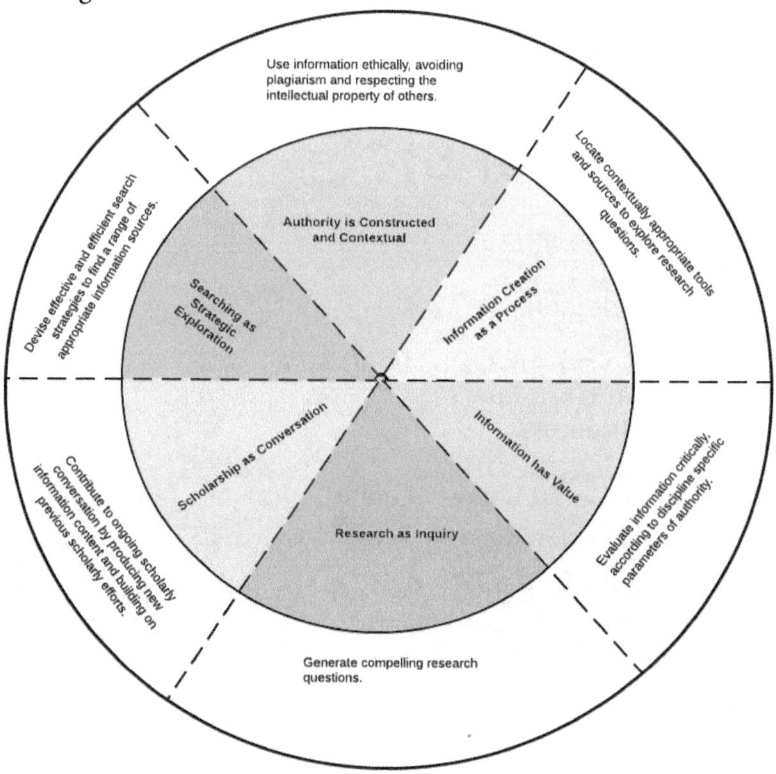

Figure 1.1: Mapping the Framework, Student Learning Outcomes, and Assignments for Information Literacy Teaching and Learning.

Source: Jannette Finch and Jolanda P. van Arnhem, "Mapping the Framework, Student Learning Outcomes, and Assignments for Information Literacy Teaching and Learning," Creative Commons Attribution-NonCommercial 4.0 International License by J. Finch and J.P. van Arnhem, College of Charleston Libraries.

Pedagogy: Metaliteracy

Metaliterate learners, as defined by Mackey and Jacobson, are characterized by practicing continual learning to adapt to a constantly evolving, information-rich environment.[4] As a learner develops metaliteracy through activities defined by four domains—behavioral, cognitive, affective, and metacognitive—they meet goals that reflect the complexity of the current information landscape.[5] Adopting the philosophy that the instructors were developing metaliterate learners changed the tone of the class, the pedagogical style, the curriculum, and assignments. The goal of the class became to encourage students to become reflective creators of their own learning, which represented a philosophical shift from a skills-based, finite learning experience to a multi-format, multi-source, multi-platform environment that included concepts of privacy, intellectual property, collaborative work, global societies, and lifelong learning.

ACRL Information Literacy Frame: Research as Inquiry

In order to begin the research process, the students had historically been asked to identify a topic they would research for the remainder of the course. The students invariably chose the same topics every semester: abortion, skateboarding on city streets, and legalizing marijuana. In selecting these subjects, students were limiting themselves in the "process of inquiry,"[6] an important piece of the frame, Research as Inquiry.

Researching skateboarding on city streets is a local issue, requiring students to locate and search inconsistently archived local papers and the formidable city code of laws. Their research could not really progress beyond sharing an opinion bolstered by limited sources. Although the topics of abortion and of legalizing marijuana give opportunity to explore bias, to verify legitimate sources about polarizing issues, and to identify sources well-suited to controversial topics, the instructors wanted students to expand their horizons of inquiry and have the opportunity to "refine research questions."[7]

To help students broaden their topic choices, instructors needed to introduce a new launching point. In 2011, author Finch attended The Teaching Professor Conference, organized by Magna Publications, which although designed for face-to-face teaching, offered many useful instructional ideas that could be modified for an online environment. In one session, Wendy Wagner, a professor at Johnson & Wales University, introduced using the popular TED Talks series (http://www.ted.com/) as a research prompt in a session titled, "When TED Talks, Everyone Learns."

The talks are succinct and the topics are often reflective of important real-world or highly relatable issues and are presented by well-qualified experts and interesting leaders. The series is diverse and far-ranging, offering students a banquet of research areas relevant to them.

In using a talk from an expert, students are challenged to think critically about the topic, and their research becomes "open-ended exploration" as they exercise "intellectual curiosity" in "developing questions" to "assess for gaps and weaknesses."[8] Each of these elements are examples of knowledge practices and dispositions of learners within the frame, Research as Inquiry.[9] A visual representation emphasizing focus on the frame, Research as Inquiry, is seen in figure 1.2.

Figure 1.2: Frame Focus: Research as Inquiry

Source: Jannette Finch and Jolanda P. van Arnhem, "Frame Focus: Research as Inquiry," Creative Commons Attribution-NonCommercial 4.0 International License by J. Finch and J.P. van Arnhem, College of Charleston Libraries.

Learning Theory: Constructivism

Open-ended assignments to prompt students to explore gaps and areas where they can expand their research fits within the tradition of constructivist learning theory. Learning and teaching enhanced by constructivist techniques is also known as experiential learning.

Constructivist theory emerges from the theoretical roots of eighteenth-century social constructivism and is reflected in the work of psychologists Adler, Piaget, and Vygotsky, and educators Dewey, Montessori, and Freire.[10] Dewey believed that inquiry and problem solving, enhanced through respectful collaboration and furthered by self-direction and personal responsibility, would result in educative meaning.[11]

Moving students from guided instruction at the introductory levels, then advancing to more open-ended tasks is commonly called scaffolding.[12] Using a scaffolded approach allows instructors to create "personally relevant learning experiences"[13] for students that work well in a self-directed online environment. As students progress, the "scaffolding is gradually withdrawn as the learner becomes more responsible" for their own knowledge construction.[14]

The launching point assignment, the "TED Talks Summary," introduces the students to the TED Talks and asks students to identify their chosen TED Talk. Students choose a TED Talk that excites their curiosity and furthers their knowledge of a subject they select based on their own interests. The instructors find it instructive to ask students to post this assignment on a public discussion space within the learning management system (LMS) so that all students can see and hear the feedback. Instructor feedback is sometimes given in audio format, allowing the students to hear the voice of the instructor, which helps to personalize the online experience and foster a positive teaching presence.[15]

Instructor comments at this stage in the student learning experience are designed to reflect positivity in their reflection of self and suggest research strategies. Some students reveal much about themselves as they explain why they are interested in their topic, which allows for a sense of community in the online environment. Joksimović, et al., in researching social presence, find that a supportive, comfortable place to exchange ideas contributes to higher order thinking.[16]

Asked to explain why they are interested in the topic, students respond with self-reflective statements, which starts the inquiry process. Students have used the assignment to affirm themselves as "non-conforming gender queer"; to reveal that "[i]t really made me think about how wrong we often are about things that we have never tried, judging them based on our own opinions (and maybe stereotypes) that have no actual facts behind them"; and to share "[c]oming from a multiracial home, I have been given the unique opportunity of being able to look at an issue from different sides and not just looking through race-colored glasses." The insights and details the students provide form the foundation for creating tightly written research topics to explore in subsequent assignments.

In the TED Talk assignment, the student is invited to share the presenter's biographical information, which practitioners will recognize as one part of the typical checklist used for verifying the quality of a resource. Inviting students to give biographical information requires a minimal amount of digging, but it ensures students spend more than a passing glance with the content.

Students then refine their research questions using the "Identifying a Topic" assignment. The activity follows the 3-2-1 method of inquiry, also known by the acronym KWL. Students share what they *know*, what they *want* to know, and what they have *learned* (NEA).[17]

Using this type of assignment continues the constructivist theoretical approach, as it hinges on the concept of building on the students' prior knowledge. The 3-2-1 questions in this assignment were modified to provide students with the opportunity to explore gaps they could mine for their research topic. The instructors ask:

- What are the *three* most important things you have learned about your TED Talks Topic?
- What are *two* things or ideas would you like to learn more about?
- What is *one* question that is not yet answered?

Samples of student responses, before receiving any guidance from an instructor, include:

- What is the effect of income on job satisfaction?
- What are the factors that hinder early childhood language development?
- Is perception of speeches affected by rhetoric?
- Does America's historical enslavement of African-Americans affect today's justice system?
- Is insulin resistance the cause of diabetes?

- Are eyewitness testimonies a reliable source of evidence?
- What is the benign violation theory in relation to humor?

The instructors were pleased to find that implementing the revised lesson plans encouraged students to expand their research focus beyond a single-word topic to issues that affect "the community at large."[18] Designing assignments to hone nascent student interest into salient research topics reinforces the students as "active agents of their own learning."[19] It is evident that students are on their way to exercising "intellectual curiosity in developing questions,"[20] an essential piece of the frame, Research as Inquiry. Students develop sophisticated avenues of research using the lesson plans in this chapter. In exploring their topics, students are using the search process itself as part of the learning process.[21]

Lesson Plan

Learner Analysis

This lesson is designed for the typical novice learner and undergraduate student, who may not know what they are interested in until they see it. As reported in Rieh, et al., several studies have found that students overestimate their knowledge, that they "do not know what they do not know."[22]

The format works well for online learners, as the TED Talks website is intuitive and does not require any special instruction to navigate. Because the talks can be accessed through transcription and are able to be paused, stopped, or rewound, they are useful tools for English language learners, too.

Orienting Context and Prerequisites

There are no prerequisites or pre-instruction work for this class.

Instructional Context

- Students must have internet access. TED Talks are accessible across many platforms, including mobile devices.
- The instructor should have internet access.
- All participants will need headphones or speakers.
- If teaching these sessions face to face, the ideal environment would be in a computer classroom or, if using their own devices, a robust WiFi signal.

Learning Outcomes and Activities

All learning outcomes and activities in this lesson are essential. This lesson is expected to take students one hour to complete.

Learning Outcomes

As a result of this lesson, students will be able to:

1. define a beginning point of research;
2. develop a provocative research question;
3. locate and analyze background information on a research question.

Learning Activities

1. TED Talks Summary *(LO1, 60 minutes, essential)*
    - Students choose a TED Talk to summarize the content, biography of the presenter, and personal reasons for selection.
    - Students were provided with the following prompt:

> **What Is TED Talks?**
>
> TED is an acronym for Technology, Entertainment, and Design. It began in 1984 as a nonprofit devoted to "Ideas Worth Spreading."
>
> **Assignment:**
>
> Choose one of the talks available at www.ted.com, answer the questions listed below and write a summary. You should pick a talk that discusses an idea, topic or experience you find highly interesting as you will be completing later assignments based on this talk.
>
> > **Lectures, speeches, addresses, readings, and other web video presentations:**
> >
> > Speaker (last name, first name). "Title of presentation." Sponsoring organization. Date of presentation. Place of presentation (if provided). Type of presentation (Lecture).
> >
> > Bittman, Mark. "What's Wrong with What We Eat." TED. Dec. 2007. Lecture.

Summary of the Talk.

In your summary, when you quote or paraphrase the presenter in your summary, **you must provide a proper in-text citation using MLA style**, as seen in the example below. If you use a direct quotation, make sure to include quotation marks. If you use a longer quote, please use block quotes. For examples, visit https://owl.english.purdue.edu/owl/.

Example 1: During the presentation, Mark Bittman states that the family dinner has been put into a coma.

Example 2: In the 1970s, home cooking was destroyed by high-fat and flavorful foods like McNuggets and Hot Pockets (Bittman).

Please Answer the Following:

1. My Name:
2. I chose the TED Talk titled:
3. It is located at (web address or URL):
4. The presenter is (include any pertinent biographical information, such as the speaker's qualifications or expertise):
5. Please write a short paragraph explaining why you're interested in this topic. By providing a bit of detail here, you'll be able to form useful research questions.
6. MLA source citation:
7. Summary of the talk.

2. Identifying a Topic Assignment *(LO2, 30-45 minutes, essential)*
   - Using their selected TED Talk, students develop a research topic.
   - Students were provided with the following prompt:

Using the TED Talks presentation you selected to research, what sparked your curiosity? What would you like to know more about or was there any part of the presentation that you doubted and would like to verify?

I. Use the 3-2-1 Method of Inquiry to start.

1. What are the THREE most important things you have learned about your TED Talks Topic?
2. What are TWO things or ideas would you like to learn more about?
3. What is ONE question that is not yet answered?

II. Using the prompts above, state your preliminary research topic in no more than ten words:

Learning Activity: Students locate and analyze two online encyclopedias for background information on their topics.

Note: Instructors may want to provide links to both public information sources, like Infoplease (http://www.infoplease.com/encyclopedia/) or Answers.com and online encyclopedias owned by the instructor's institution. Using both provides an additional learning opportunity, as instructors may open a discussion on the differences of each type of source.

III. Next, search at least TWO online encyclopedias to locate and read background material on your topic.

IV. Now, list at least 10 words or short phrases you found **in these online encyclopedias** that could be used to search for information on your topic:

Assessment

The introductory assignments for the one-credit online information literacy class are low stakes. Because the assignments build and scaffold on each other, instructors encourage students with multiple low-risk assignments worth four to five points. As students advance, the assignments are worth more.

Rubrics may be developed requiring levels of assessment required by the instructor. For example, for an introductory assignment online, the instructor may be most interested in whether the student can follow directions. Rubrics at this level may be more formative and include:

- The student followed guidelines for submitting the assignment.
- The student provided an accurate web address for the TED Talk so I could access it.
- The student was able to summarize the main points of the TED Talk.
- The student provided a correctly formatted source citation for the talk using MLA format.

A simple grading rubric can help the student embrace the self-directed learning necessary in an online class. As the assignments build, the elements of the rubric reflect more faith in the student's initiative. See Appendix 1A for a sample grading rubric for Learning Activity One and Learning Activity Two.

Online Resources

- Scaffolding Instruction Using the *Framework*, Units of Study, Student Learning Outcomes, and Sample Assignments, https://goo.gl/U4EJRA.
- Scaffolding Instruction Using the *Framework*, Units of Study, Student Learning Outcomes Worksheet, https://goo.gl/AsE38J.

Appendix 1A

Sample Grading Rubric: Learning Activity One

The student followed guidelines for submitting the assignment. (1 Point)	__Agree (1 Point) __Neither Agree nor Disagree (.5 Point) __Disagree (0 Point)
The student provided an accurate web address for the TED Talk so I could access it. (1 Point)	__Agree (1 Point) __Neither Agree nor Disagree (.5 Point) __Disagree (0 Point)
The student was able to summarize the main points of the TED Talk. (1 Point)	__Agree (1 Point) __Neither Agree nor Disagree (.5 Point) __Disagree (0 Point)
The student provided a correctly formatted source citation for the talk using MLA format. (1 Point)	__Agree (1 Point) __Neither Agree nor Disagree (.5 Point) __Disagree (0 Point)

Sample Grading Rubric: Learning Activity Two

The student answered the 3-2-1 inquiry questions. (1 Point)	__Agree (1 Point) __Neither Agree nor Disagree (.5 Point) __Disagree (0 Point)
The student stated a researchable topic. (1 Point)	__Agree (1 Point) __Neither Agree nor Disagree (.5 Point) __Disagree (0 Point)
The student found relevant background information for the topic. (1 Point)	__Agree (1 Point) __Neither Agree nor Disagree (.5 Point) __Disagree (0 Point)
The student listed terms and phrases that will be useful to research. (1 Point)	__Agree (1 Point) __Neither Agree nor Disagree (.5 Point) __Disagree (0 Point)

Notes

1. American Library Association, *Framework for Information Literacy for Higher Education*, ACRL: Guidelines, Standards, and Frameworks (February 2015). http://www.ala.org/acrl/standards/ilframework.
2. Allison Hosier, Daryl Bullis, Deborah Bernnard, Greg Bobish, Irina Holden, Jenna Hecker, Tor Loney, and Trudi Jacobson, *The Information Literacy User's Guide: An Open, Online Textbook,* eds. Greg Bobish and Trudi Jacobson (Open SUNY Textbooks, 2014), http://textbooks.

opensuny.org/the-information-literacy-users-guide-an-open-online-textbook/; SCONUL Working Group on Information Literacy, *The SCONUL Seven Pillars of Information Literacy: Core Model for Higher Education*, April 2011, accessed February 26, 2017, https://www.sconul.ac.uk/sites/default/files/documents/coremodel.pdf.
3. "The Community of Inquiry," *Community of Inquiry*, https://coi.athabascau.ca/. This shift in focus for teaching librarians is also appearing in the field of librarianship with the adoption of the ACRL Framework in 2015, as noted by the emerging revisions to the 2007 Standards and Proficiencies for Instruction Librarians and Coordinators. Association of College and Research Libraries, "Roles and Strengths of Teaching Librarians," American Library Association, last modified 2017, accessed September 14, 2017, http://www.ala.org/acrl/standards/teachinglibrarians.
4. Tom Mackey and Trudi Jacobson, "Goals and Learning Objectives," Metaliteracy.org, September 11, 2014, http://metaliteracy.org/learning-objectives.
5. Ibid.
6. American Library Association, *Framework for Information Literacy for Higher Education.*
7. Ibid.
8. Ibid.
9. Ibid.
10. William Williamson, "Assessing Constructivist Elements in the Online Learning Environment (PhD diss, University of North Carolina, Chapel Hill, 2010).
11. Karen Swan, D. R. Garrison, and Jennifer C. Richardson, "A Constructivist Approach to Online Learning: The Community of Inquiry Framework," in *Information Technology and Constructivism in Higher Education: Progressive Learning Frameworks*, ed. C. R. Payne (Hershey, PA: IGI Global), 45.
12. Rachel Spronken-Smith and Rebecca Walker, "Can Inquiry-Based Learning Strengthen the Links Between Teaching and Disciplinary Research?" *Studies in Higher Education* 35, no. 6 (2010): 726, doi: 10.1080/03075070903315502.
13. Cosette Armstrong, "In the Zone: Vygotskian-Inspired Pedagogy for Sustainability," *Journal of Classroom Interaction* 50, no. 2 (2015): 135.
14. Ibid.
15. Jannette Finch and Renée N. Jefferson, "Designing Authentic Learning Tasks for Online Library Instruction," *The Journal of Academic Librarianship* 39, no. 2 (2013): 187.
16. Srećko Joksimović, Dragan Gašević, Vitomir Kovanović, Bernhard E. Riecke, and Marek Hatala. "Social Presence in Online Discussions as a Process Predictor of Academic Performance," *Journal of Computer Assisted Learning* 31, no. 6 (2015): 640.
17. NEA: National Education Association, "K-W-L (Know, Want to Know, Learned)," *National Education Association*, http://www.nea.org/tools/k-w-l-know-want-to-know-learned.html.
18. American Library Association.
19. Melissa Wallace, "Team-Based Learning in Introductory Translation Courses," in *Handbook of Research on Teaching Methods in Language Translation and Interpretation*, eds. Ying Cui and Wei Zhao (IGI Global, 2015): 29.
20. American Library Association.
21. Soo Young Rieh, Kevyn Collins-Thompson, Preben Hansen, and Hye-Jung Lee, "Towards Searching as a Learning Process: A Review of Current Perspectives and Future Directions," *Journal of Information Science* 42, no. 1 (2016): 25.
22. Ibid., 22.

Bibliography

American Library Association. *Framework for Information Literacy for Higher Education.* ACRL: Guidelines, Standards, and Frameworks. (February 2015). http://www.ala.org/acrl/standards/ilframework.

Armstrong, Cosette. "In the Zone: Vygotskian-Inspired Pedagogy for Sustainability." *Journal of Classroom Interaction* 50, no. 2 (2015): 133–44.

Association of College and Research Libraries. "Roles and Strengths of Teaching Librarians." American Library Association. Last modified 2017. Accessed September 14, 2017. http://www.ala.org/acrl/standards/teachinglibrarians.

"The Community of Inquiry." *Community of Inquiry*. https://coi.athabascau.ca/.

Finch, Jannette L., and Renée N. Jefferson. "Designing Authentic Learning Tasks for Online Library Instruction." *The Journal of Academic Librarianship* 39, no. 2 (2013): 181–88.

Finch, Jannette, and Jolanda van Arnhem. *Mapping the Framework, Student Learning Outcomes, and Assignments for Information Literacy Teaching and Learning.* Creative Commons Attribution-NonCommercial 4.0 International License by J. Finch and J.P. van Arnhem, College of Charleston Libraries.

Finch, Jannette, and Jolanda van Arnhem. "Frame Focus: Research as Inquiry." Creative Commons Attribution-NonCommercial 4.0 International License by J. Finch and J.P. van Arnhem, College of Charleston Libraries.

Hosier, Allison, Daryl Bullis, Deborah Bernnard, Greg Bobish, Irina Holden, Jenna Hecker, Tor Loney, and Trudi Jacobson. *The Information Literacy User's Guide: An Open, Online Textbook,* edited by Greg Bobish and Trudi Jacobson. Open SUNY Textbooks, 2014. http://textbooks.opensuny.org/the-information-literacy-users-guide-an-open-online-textbook/.

Joksimović, Srećko, Dragan Gašević, Vitomir Kovanović, Bernhard E. Riecke, and Marek Hatala. "Social Presence in Online Discussions as a Process Predictor of Academic Performance." *Journal of Computer Assisted Learning* 31, no. 6 (2015): 638–54.

Mackey, Tom, and Trudi Jacobson. "Goals and Learning Objectives," Metaliteracy.org. September 11, 2014. http://metaliteracy.org/learning-objectives/.

NEA: National Education Association. "K-W-L (Know, Want to Know, Learned)." *National Education Association.* http://www.nea.org/tools/k-w-l-know-want-to-know-learned.html.

Rieh, Soo Young, Kevyn Collins-Thompson, Preben Hansen, and Hye-Jung Lee. "Towards Searching as a Learning Process: A Review of Current Perspectives and Future Directions." *Journal of Information Science* 42, no. 1 (2016): 19–34. doi: 10.1177/0165551515615841.

Swan, Karen, D. R. Garrison, and Jennifer C. Richardson. "A Constructivist Approach to Online Learning: The Community of Inquiry Framework." In *Information Technology and Constructivism in Higher Education: Progressive Learning Frameworks,* edited by C.R. Payne, 43–57. Hershey, PA: IGI Global, 2009.

Spronken-Smith, Rachel, and Rebecca Walker. "Can Inquiry-Based Learning Strengthen the Links Between Teaching and Disciplinary Research?" *Studies in Higher Education* 35, no. 6 (2010): 723–40. doi: 10.1080/03075070903315502.

Wallace, Melissa. "Team-Based Learning in Introductory Translation Courses." In *Handbook of Research on Teaching Methods in Language Translation and Interpretation,* edited by Ying Cui and Wei Zhao. IGI Global, 2015.

Williamson, William. "Assessing Constructivist Elements in the Online Learning Environment." PhD diss, University of North Carolina, Chapel Hill, 2010.

CHAPTER 2

A Bird's Eye View of the Research Process:

Developing Students' Attention to Research Practices, Iterations, and Inquiry

Jennifer Jarson
Head Librarian
Pennsylvania State University-Lehigh Valley

ACRL Information Literacy Frame: Research as Inquiry
Discipline: Multidisciplinary
Subject: Interdisciplinary
Pedagogy: Self-Regulated Learning
Special Population: Undergraduate Students

This lesson asks students to uncover and reflect on their research practices and attitudes and, more specifically, how iterations in the research process can play a valuable role in driving inquiry. In the first component of this lesson plan, students draw a visual representation such as a flowchart, outline, or illustration that characterizes their typical research process. Activity directions ask them to include steps they took, where they changed direction or encountered problems, and emotions they felt as they progressed in the process. These drawings serve as a useful launching pad for conversations about the paths research can take, how we engage in and approach research, specific research strategies, and the benefits of iterations in research. By taking a bird's eye view of the research process, students become more attentive to and reflective about their research practices, especially how research can inform and drive their questions and ideas.

This lesson can help instructors reveal and shape students' expectations about the research process. For example, students sometimes feel overwhelmed by or anxious about research. The activities described here can expose the component parts of the research process, demystifying it and making it feel more manageable to students. By starting to recognize that the twists and turns they may see as frustrating stumbling blocks or even failures are in fact valuable waypoints that propel their research and understanding forward, students may reduce their frustration and anxiety about the research process.

Because this lesson helps make students' research experiences more visible to them, it provides opportunities for reflection on their research behaviors and strategies, as well as their emotional responses. By revealing how students approach and conceive of the research process, these activities can serve as a formative assessment, or informal diagnostic test, helping students themselves and instructors identify misunderstandings, challenges, and frustrations.

"Playable, not just performable": Uncovering what's hidden

I recently read Carrie Brownstein's memoir and was struck by a particular passage in which she reflected on some of the key experiences of her adolescence that helped shape her as a musician.[1] She first described how invigorated and enthralled she felt as a young girl in stadium-sized crowds watching pop music giants Madonna and George Michael perform. The spectacle of these performances entranced and inspired Brownstein but also made them opaque and feel unattainable. "The music was in the room and in my body," she wrote, "yet I had no idea how it had been assembled or how to break it apart.... I remained merely a fan ...with no means of claiming the sounds as my own."[2] In those massive crowds, she remained an onlooker with no discernible entry point for her own participation.

Brownstein went on to describe her experiences a few years later attending far less grandiose rock and punk shows. At these mostly smaller venues, Brownstein could get close to the musicians and observe their techniques and interactions. Here the making of the music and the performances' component parts were visible. "It seems obvious," Brownstein reflected, "but it was the first time I realized that music was playable, not just performable—that it had a process and a seed, a beginning, middle, and end."[3] The proximity and transparency made the music and the performances feel more accessible and attainable. Brownstein could see a path for herself in the music.

While worlds apart in some ways, the parallels between Brownstein's experience and information literacy development are rather striking to me. Brownstein's reflection did not inspire the lesson described here per se, but it does represent the inspiration behind it. Her account showcases the power of uncovering process. Her reflection on the opacity of the extravagant concerts versus the transparency of the small shows illuminates the kinds of disconnects our students also experience in their academic lives. When the process of making and performing music was revealed for her, Brownstein could then imagine it for herself. Similarly, to leave the component parts and mechanics of research unseen and unspoken—to show our students only final published journal articles polished by experts or rehearsed and perfected search strategies, for example—is to leave the door closed for many. I am recalling the students I have worked with who are ready to abandon their research questions because their first search does not turn up perfect matches, or the students who are overwhelmed by the pile of articles before them with no plan for how to organize, read, and make sense of them. For these students, our conversations about process and strategy opened paths forward and transformed their perspectives. We must help our students uncover, develop, articulate, and reflect on process. To reveal inner workings and rough edges opens the door to participation and empowers our students.

ACRL Information Literacy Frame: Research as Inquiry

The lesson described in this chapter aligns with Research as Inquiry, one of the six core concepts in the Association of College and Research Libraries' *Framework for Information Literacy for Higher Education*.[4] This concept, or frame, focuses on the importance of asking and pursuing questions and brings the notion of process to the foreground. The value of uncovering process in order to advance one's understanding of a topic or question is especially evident in the frame's "knowledge practices." In order to effectively pursue a question, for example, learners may break it into its component parts. Gaps identified during research help learners ask questions. Organizing and synthesizing information they have gathered helps learners make meaning as well as identify further questions.

The frame also underscores the iterative nature of the research process. Understanding the research process as iterative, and iterations as valuable and productive in identifying and pursuing questions, requires a variety of "dispositions," including an open-minded attitude, persistence, and flexibility. These practices and habits of mind suggest that learners' awareness of and attention to the process of research can propel their understanding of an area forward and advance their inquiry.

Metacognition, then, surfaces throughout the *Framework* and is especially notable in the Research as Inquiry frame. A metacognitive mindset refers to an "awareness and understanding of one's own thought processes ...focus[ing] on how people learn and process information, taking into consideration people's awareness of how they learn."[5] The knowledge practices and dispositions articulated in this frame prioritize learners' awareness of and reflection on the purpose, strategy, and path of the research process. Whether we are considering Brownstein's musical development or our students' research, uncovering and reflecting on process can help learners navigate and manage it and tolerate its ambiguity.

Pedagogy: Self-regulated Learning

This lesson draws students' attention to the research process. By articulating their research behaviors and attitudes, the lesson aims to promote their metacognitive awareness and reflective practice about the research process, their understanding of how research can drive inquiry, as well as recognition of their agency in the process. Self-regulated learning theory informs the lesson outlined in this chapter, bolstering the practices and dispositions detailed in the Research as Inquiry frame.

Self-regulated learning refers to the behaviors and attitudes that help students succeed and become self-directed in their learning. It is "the voice in your head that asks you questions about your learning. More formally, self-regulated learning is the conscious planning, monitoring, evaluation, and ultimately control of one's learning in order to maximize it.... It means being mindful, intentional, reflective, introspective, self-aware, self-controlled, and self-disciplined about learning."[6] Self-regulated learning theory suggests that these self-monitoring and reflective practices and habits of mind, rather than content knowledge and intelligence alone, are critical to achievement.[7]

The literature generally categorizes the major aspects of self-regulated learning as motivational, behavioral, emotional, and metacognitive.[8] Self-regulated learners, then, monitor, reflect on, evaluate, and adjust not only their cognitive processes but also their emotions, behaviors, and environment.[9] They recognize learning as something they are proactively doing rather than something that happens to them passively.[10] Self-regulated learning supports students' development as active agents in their own learning.

As might be expected, developing self-regulation abilities is a long-term process and is likely the result of both formal instruction and informal expectations and environmental conditions, ranging from direct instruction to modeling to corrective feedback to cooperative learning to setting expectations for self-directed behaviors.[11] The literature suggests that formal "interventions," or teaching activities, may take a wide variety of shapes, whether short-term or long-term, focused on single or multiple strategies, or specific to a particular subject area or more general.[12] "Wrappers," or small activities surrounding an existing assignment, like the one described in this chapter, are one kind of minor intervention to help students practice self-monitoring and reflection.[13]

Lesson Plan

Learner Analysis

- This lesson asks students to create a visual representation of their research process and discuss other visual representations. Some students may welcome the chance to express their work and thinking visually or aesthetically, while others may feel challenged by it. It may be worth emphasizing for students how flexible the notion of "visual representation" is (e.g., drawing, flowchart, outline, etc.) and reminding students that they are not being evaluated on their aesthetic sensibilities or artistic abilities.

- While making a visual representation and viewing other visual representations are the crux of this lesson, it could be modified for students with visual impairments by replacing the drawing/viewing activities with discussion prompts.

Orienting Context and Prerequisites

- This lesson does not require any pre-instruction learner tasks.

Instructional Context

- Instructors will need to prepare the drawing activity directions for students (as seen in figure 2.1), as well as sample visual representations of the research process (as seen in figures 2.2 and 2.3). It is likely easiest for instructors to prepare these materials in advance of class and compile them into a slideshow (e.g., in PowerPoint) or the like. In addition to facilitating in-class use, these materials can then be easily shared in the learning management system (e.g., Canvas or Blackboard) for students' later reference, if appropriate. However, if instructors do not have access to a computer, projector, and screen in the classroom, the activity directions can be posted to a whiteboard or given verbally and the sample images can be drawn on the whiteboard during class time.

Learning Outcomes and Activities

Outcomes

1. Students will describe and interpret their research processes in order to understand how their behaviors, obstacles, attitudes, and emotions affect it.
2. Students will identify patterns and themes generally and instances of iterations, difficulty, and affect specifically in their representations in order to monitor and reflect on their research processes.
3. Students will describe characteristics of research as a linear process versus research as an iterative process in order to understand how research informs inquiry.

Learning Activities

Notes on timing

Altogether, the essential activities in this lesson can take as little as twenty minutes. The lesson can easily be integrated into a fifty- to seventy-five-minute, one-shot information literacy session, as well as in other settings. Because the activity focuses on the research process overall, it can align with sessions designed to focus on different phases of a research assignment. The activity aligns well, for example, with sessions scheduled at the outset of a research project where the focus might be on finding and narrowing topics/questions. The lesson can also fit well with sessions scheduled further into a research project when students have already identified topics/questions of interest and perhaps even begun gathering information. In that case, the lesson might serve as a useful way for students to monitor and reflect on their learning and/or to redirect students' attention to the iterative nature of research generally and the potential for still further flexibility and revision in their continuing work.

1. Facilitate research process drawing activity *(LO1, 5–10 minutes, essential)*
    - As the first component of the activity, students create a representation of key elements in their research processes, including the steps they took, where they changed direction or encountered problems, and emotions they felt. See figure 2.1 for a sample activity prompt for students.
        - ▷ Instructors may choose to permit students flexibility in creating their representations. The directions in figure 2.1, for example, enable students to create representations in any form (e.g., pictorial, narrative, or a combination) and to include any/all research process phases and features they choose. This flexibility can make the activity more accessible to students and be particularly revealing for instructors as it gives students wide berth to express their processes in the ways that make the most sense to them.
        - ▷ If the pedagogical context requires more focus, instructors may choose to specify the form and features of the representations. Such specificity may help instructors and students concentrate on a particular aspect or phase of the research process, such as identifying a topic, refining

a topic, or searching for sources. More specific directions may also provide consistency across student work for comparison or evaluation and therefore better meet particular pedagogical needs.

Figure 2.1: Sample research process drawing prompt

What will your library research process look like?

Draw a representation (e.g., picture/illustration, outline, flow chart, or diagram) that you think depicts what your library research process will be for this project. You might think back to a past library research experience or what you generally do as a guide, or you might portray what you hope you will do this time. Your representation might include steps you will take (forward and/or backward), key moments of discovery or understanding you anticipate, the way you expect you will feel at key points, etc.

2. Reflect on and discuss drawing activity *(LO2, 5–10 minutes, essential)*
   - Students' research process representations then serve as a jumping off point for conversation about the research process. Students will identify particular aspects or themes in their representations, facilitated through class discussion. The prompts in figure 2.2 may be useful in guiding discussion with students to reflect generally on themes or patterns in their representations and/or call attention specifically to instances of iterations, difficulty, and affect.

Figure 2.2: Sample discussion prompts

1. As you made your representation, what did you notice or think about?
2. Do you notice any patterns in your representation?
3. Is your representation forward moving only? Did you include any moments where you circled back or changed course?
4. Did you include any problem spots in your representation?
5. Did you include any emotions or feelings in your representation?

3. Discuss research as a linear versus iterative process (*LO3, 5–10 minutes, essential*)
   - In the class discussion about their representations, students may already begin to talk about iterations in their research. Even if they do not identify iterative moments in their representations, the activity can serve as a useful launching pad to introduce the idea of iterative research. To begin, instructors may introduce a drawing that represents research as a linear process, like the one in figure 2.3. Students will characterize what about the drawing is "linear," facilitated through class discussion. Note, for example, that the research process in this representation might be characterized as linear because it only moves forward. The process never changes direction, never doubles back; the research does not inform inquiry.

Figure 2.3: Research as a linear process

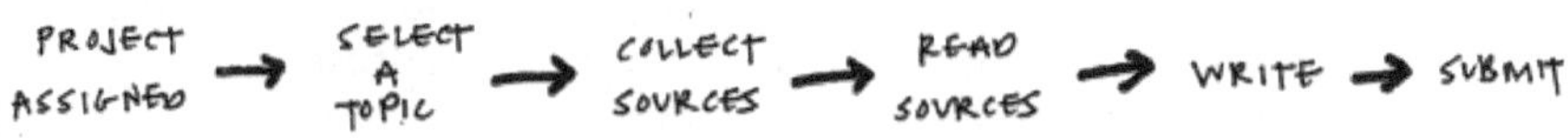

   - Instructors will next introduce a representation that represents research as an iterative process, like the one in figure 2.4, and describe the steps depicted in the representation. Students will define the word "iterative" or "iteration" and characterize what about the representation is iterative, facilitated through class discussion. In figure 2.4, for example, a research project is assigned and the student chooses a topic but begins to test the viability of the topic and refine the topic based on initial research. The student proceeds to reading and organizing sources and in so doing may further expand or narrow the topic and perhaps find additional information sources. The student begins to write and revise. Even at this stage, a student may still be negotiating the scope of inquiry, discard some information sources, or perhaps identify information gaps that need to be filled. By calling special attention to the various iterative moments represented throughout the drawing (e.g., as indicated with arrows in figure 2.4), students will notice where the process informs and drives inquiry.

Figure 2.4: Research as an iterative process

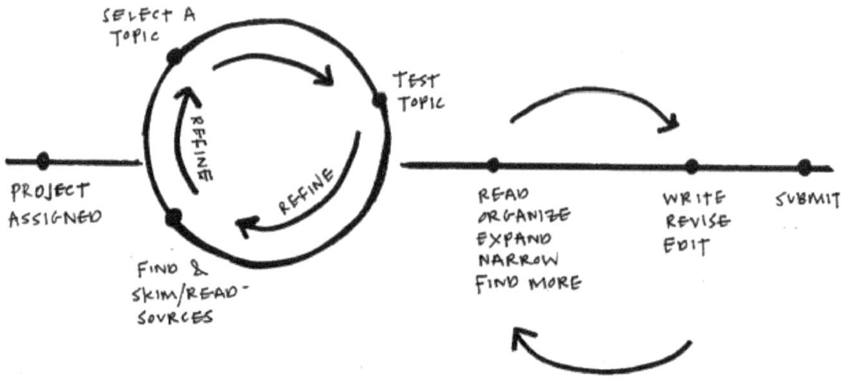

This representation is adapted from Sarah Crissinger's blog post, "Being 'Human' In the Classroom: A Case for Personal Testimony in Pedagogy," for ACRLog (http://acrlog.org/2015/10/14/being-human-in-the-classroom/).

- Students will compare and contrast the representations of linear and iterative research, facilitated through class discussion.

Learning Activity Variations for more embedded instructional contexts (optional)

1. After completing their projects, students create a second representation of their research process, this time specific to the project they just completed. Students can compare their initial drawing and final drawing, facilitated through in-class discussion or by writing a short reflection, in order to deepen their reflection on and metacognition about their learning.
2. Students create representations of their research processes at different stages throughout a project, focusing in on particular moments, phases, or challenges, to help them monitor and reflect on their learning in the moment. Facilitated in-class discussions or short written reflection assignments may help students make meaning of their various representations.

Assessment

Formative assessment

In creating their representations, students' attention is drawn to their own research processes. The ensuing in-class conversations about the activity, followed by discussion about research as a linear versus iterative process, help students further reflect on their own processes. As such, the activity serves as a formative assessment for students, helping them monitor, diagnose, and adjust their own learning.

Similarly, the drawing activity and its accompanying in-class conversations can serve as a formative assessment of student understanding and learning for instructors. Noticing the themes and patterns students represent and identify in their drawings informs instructors about students' behaviors and metacognitive awareness, helping the instructor respond to and redirect students.

If students create follow-up drawing activities as described in the variations section above, there are still further opportunities for them to evaluate their work and potentially their change in understanding of the research process. Those comparative reflections and evaluations can be facilitated by in-class discussions, writing assignments, etc.

Formalizing formative assessment

Should instructors want to make this formative assessment more formalized, a few options to consider include journaling and coding. Instructors may use a reflective teaching journal to document and reflect on the in-class discussion. Instructors might note in their journals individual students' reactions and comments or the patterns and themes across students' reactions and comments. Journaling can direct the instructor's attention, much like drawing can direct students' attention.[14]

For a more detailed and systematic assessment, instructors might consider gathering students' drawings and coding their work for particular instances or themes. For example, instructors might count instances of iterations present in each student's representation or categorize the nature of the iterations (e.g., iterations in topic development, source selection, or writing). Alternately, instructors may respond to themes that emerge from students' drawings, rather than look for instances of predetermined codes or categories.

Assessing student growth

If the instructor has the opportunity to implement this activity in an embedded context, further opportunities for assessment of student learning may be available. Instructors may be able to evaluate changes, for example, in students' learning, behavior, and metacognition by coding and comparing their first and later drawings or by evaluating students in-class discussions and/or written reflections on their own comparisons of first and final drawings.

Notes

1. I first explored using this excerpt from Carrie Brownstein's memoir to talk about information literacy in a blog post, "'Playable, Not Just Performable': Telling the Story of Information Literacy," for ACRLog (http://acrlog.org/2016/06/07/playable-not-just-performable-telling-the-story-of-information-literacy/).
2. Carrie Brownstein, *Hunger Makes Me a Modern Girl: A Memoir* (New York: Riverhead Books, 2015), 7.
3. Brownstein, *Hunger Makes Me a Modern Girl*, 8–9.
4. Association of College and Research Libraries, *Framework for Information Literacy for Higher Education*, last updated January 11, 2016, http://www.ala.org/acrl/standards/ilframework.
5. Association of College and Research Libraries, "Framework."
6. Linda B. Nilson, "The Secret of Self-Regulated Learning," *Faculty Focus*, June 16, 2014, http://www.facultyfocus.com/articles/teaching-and-learning/secret-self-regulated-learning/.
7. Linda B. Nilson, *Creating Self-Regulated Learners: Strategies to Strengthen Students' Self-Awareness and Learning Skills* (Sterling, VA: Stylus, 2013), 2–4.
8. For example, Barry J. Zimmerman, "Self-Regulated Learning and Academic Achievement: An Overview," *Educational Psychologist*, 25, no. 1 (1990): 4–5; Linda B. Nilson, *Creating Self-Regulated Learners*, 5; Anastasia Efklides, "Interactions of Metacognition with Motivations and Affect in Self-Regulated Learning: The MASRL Model," *Educational Psychologist* 46 no. 1 (2011): 6.
9. Nilson, *Creating Self-Regulated Learners*, 5.
10. Barry J. Zimmerman, "Becoming a Self-Regulated Learner: An Overview," *Theory Into Practice*, 41, no. 2 (2002): 65.
11. Barry J. Zimmerman, "Developing Self-Fulfilling Cycles of Academic Regulation: An Analysis of Exemplary Instructional Models," in *Self-Regulated Learning: From Teaching to Self-Reflective Practice*, ed. Dale H. Schunk and Barry J. Zimmerman (New York: Guilford Press, 1998), 10–11.
12. For example, Nilson, *Creating Self-Regulated Learners*; Barbara K. Hofer, Shirley L. Yu, and Paul R. Pintrich, "Teaching College Students to Be Self-Regulated Learners," in *Self-Regulated Learning: From Teaching to Self-Reflective Practice*, ed. Dale H. Schunk and Barry J. Zimmerman (New York: Guilford Press, 1998).
13. Marsha C. Lovett, "Teaching Metacognition," (presentation at EDUCAUSE, January 29, 2008), https://events.educause.edu/ir/library/pdf/ELI08104.pdf; Carol Ormand, "Teaching Metacognition," accessed February 10, 2017, http://serc.carleton.edu/NAGTWorkshops/metacognition/teaching_metacognition.html; Eveline Houtman, "'Mind-Blowing:' Fostering Self-Regulated Learning in Information Literacy Instruction," *Communications in Information Literacy*, 9, no. 1 (2015).
14. For more on the practice of keeping a reflective teaching journal, see Elizabeth K. Tompkins, "A Reflective Teaching Journal: An Instructional Improvement Tool for Academic Librarians," *College & Undergraduate Libraries*, 16, no. 4 (2009).

Bibliography

Association of College and Research Libraries. *Framework for Information Literacy for Higher Education.* Last modified January 11, 2016. http://www.ala.org/acrl/standards/ilframework.

Brownstein, Carrie. *Hunger Makes Me a Modern Girl: A Memoir.* New York: Riverhead Books, 2015.

Crissinger, Sarah. "Being 'Human' in the Classroom: A Case for Personal Testimony in Pedagogy." ACRLog blog, October 14, 2015. http://acrlog.org/2015/10/14/being-human-in-the-classroom/.

Efklides, Anastasia. "Interactions of Metacognition with Motivations and Affect in Self-Regulated Learning: The MASRL Model." *Educational Psychologist* 46 no. 1 (2011): 6–25.

Hofer, Barbara K., Shirley L. Yu, and Paul R. Pintrich. "Teaching College Students to Be Self-Regulated Learners." In *Self-Regulated Learning: From Teaching to Self-Reflective Practice*, edited by Dale H. Schunk and Barry J. Zimmerman, 57–85. New York: Guilford Press, 1998.

Houtman, Eveline. "'Mind-Blowing': Fostering Self-Regulated Learning in Information Literacy Instruction." *Communications in Information Literacy* 9, no. 1 (2015): 6–18.

Lovett, Marsha C. "Teaching Metacognition." Presentation at EDUCAUSE, January 29, 2008. https://events.educause.edu/ir/library/pdf/ELI08104.pdf.

Nilson, Linda B. *Creating Self-Regulated Learners: Strategies to Strengthen Students' Self-Awareness and Learning Skills.* Sterling, VA: Stylus, 2013.

________. "The Secret of Self-Regulated Learning." *Faculty Focus*, June 16, 2014. http://www.facultyfocus.com/articles/teaching-and-learning/secret-self-regulated-learning/.

Ormand, Carol. "Teaching Metacognition." Accessed February 10, 2017. http://serc.carleton.edu/NAGTWorkshops/metacognition/teaching_metacognition.html.

Tompkins, Elizabeth K. "A Reflective Teaching Journal: An Instructional Improvement Tool for Academic Librarians." *College & Undergraduate Libraries*, 16, no. 4 (2009): 221–38.

Zimmerman, Barry J. "Self-Regulated Learning and Academic Achievement: An Overview." *Educational Psychologist*, 25, no. 1 (1990): 3–17.

________. "Developing Self-Fulfilling Cycles of Academic Regulation: An Analysis of Exemplary Instructional Models." In *Self-Regulated Learning: From Teaching to Self-Reflective Practice*, edited by Dale H. Schunk and Barry J. Zimmerman, 1–19. New York: Guilford Press, 1998.

________. "Becoming a Self-Regulated Learner: An Overview." *Theory Into Practice*, 41, no. 2 (2002): 64–70.

CHAPTER 3

Change is Hard:
Using Conceptual Change Theory to Promote "Research as Inquiry"

Kimberly Miller
Learning Technologies Librarian
Towson University

ACRL Information Literacy Frame: Research as Inquiry
Discipline: Multidisciplinary
Subject: Research process
Learning Theory: Conceptual Change Theory
Special Population: First-Year Students

Every so often during library instruction sessions, I overhear professors advise their first-year students to "trust the process." Students are asked to "trust" that each step of their scaffolded, semester-long research project will lead them where they want to go. Similarly, the *Framework for Information Literacy for Higher Education* challenges librarians to help students see "Research as Inquiry."[1] We encourage students to use information to iteratively ask and answer interesting questions; however, this approach conflicts with the mental picture of the research process that students bring with them to college. Students may instead struggle to understand the relevance of what can look like a drawn-out and repetitive process, preferring to rely on a more linear approach that has worked well for them in the past. In response, this chapter shares a two-part blended lesson, grounded in conceptual change theory, designed to nudge first-year students toward an iterative research process.

ACRL Information Literacy Frame: Research as Inquiry

"Research as Inquiry" describes research as "iterative and depend[ent] upon asking increasingly complex or new questions whose answers in turn develop additional questions or lines of inquiry in any field."[2] Ideally, this means students learn to view research as an iterative process that requires deep engagement with the information environment, allowing questions and answers to guide their studies. However, based on their previous experiences, expectations, and motivations about college-level research, novice students instead see research as moving in a straight path from idea to final product as quickly as possible. They may skip early stages of the research process,[3] stop looking for information when they feel they have a correct amount rather than when they have sufficiently used the information to refine a question,[4] and collect just enough sources to earn a good grade.[5] This approach conflicts with the goals of Research as Inquiry, and means that library instruction needs to encourage students to critically examine their existing mental models of the research process before considering how new approaches may help them answer increasingly complex questions.

Learning Theory: Conceptual Change

"Conceptual change" is one theory librarians may use to understand how and why students change their mental models of the research process. Conceptual change theory proposes that learners create new knowledge when they actively engage with their prior experiences and alter their underlying conceptual frameworks, or "structured mental representations."[6] While change may be as simple as incorporating new knowledge into existing mental models, it is unlikely that students' "naïve conceptions" reflect an expert's understanding.[7] Instead, learning requires modifying existing concepts, or creating entirely new concepts, to account for new knowledge. Conceptual change theory is also helpful while working with the framework because threshold concepts are overarching conceptual understandings that change the way we understand a discipline.[8] Crossing a threshold may also be understood as undergoing conceptual change.[9] In the frame Research as Inquiry, students should grasp the concept that research is a non-linear process that requires using a variety of information sources to ask and answer complex questions.

In conceptual change, learners must first uncover and become dissatisfied with their initial mental concept.[10] Students explore their existing mental representations and discover why knowledge gaps are cause for concern.[11] For library instruction, this means students need to explore their existing model of the research process before they can consider a new approach. Likewise, library instruction that is overly focused on new skills, like the mechanics of searching unfamiliar databases, may mistakenly confirm students' mental model of research as a linear, information-gathering task. After examining their existing mental models, students should encounter replacement concepts that are understandable, plausible, and lead to new ways of thinking.[12] Instruction that coincides with early phases of the research process and demonstrates how an iterative approach helps alleviate concerns, like topic selection anxiety, can be an opportunity to promote change in how students conceptualize the research process.

Teaching to conceptual-level information literacy objectives is not new, and tools like concept maps and analogies can be used to help overcome students' inaccurate mental models.[13] Concept maps are helpful conceptual change instructional tools because they provide learners and instructors with a tangible opportunity to engage with otherwise invisible mental models.[14] Likewise, analogies help students create a bridge between their initial concept and a new mental model.[15]

This two-part learning environment uses conceptual change theory and tools to (1) assess students' existing conceptions of the research process, (2) present a new concept aligned with Research as Inquiry, and (3) use students' research experiences to present the new concept as a viable alternative. In the first pre-instruction activity and instruction session, students create concept maps to examine their existing mental models of the research process. The second pre-instruction activity and instruction session seek to demonstrate how an iterative research process assumes new questions will shape a topic over time. Framing research as an opportunity dive into answering an interesting and flexible question should continue to ease the change process.[16]

Lesson Plan

Learner Analysis

This two-part lesson is designed for a first-year social science seminar course with twenty to twenty-five students.

- First-year students struggle through college-level research, in part, due to strategies they bring to their coursework from high school.[17]
- Developmentally, first-year students' black-and-white view of knowledge results in seeing research as a one-way, linear path of information gathering.[18]
- These expectations and behaviors conflict with Research as Inquiry's iterative process and are challenges that librarians can address during information literacy instruction.

Orienting Context and Prerequisites

This lesson is a blended learning environment with activities before and during two face-to-face instruction sessions.

- Students complete two pre-instruction online learning modules outside of class time. See "Learning Activities" for module details.
- It is helpful if the course professor allows students to earn credit for completing pre-session modules.

Instructional Context

Learning Management System (LMS)

- This lesson works best if pre-session modules are embedded within the class LMS.
- With no access to the LMS, distribute pre-session content using other common web-based tools like Google Forms or SpringShare's LibGuides.
- Create and distribute pre-session activities at least one week before each face-to-face session.

Concept Mapping Tools

- Students complete individual concept maps as part of the first pre-session module.
- There are many free, web-based concept mapping programs; however, students should be able to label and indicate the directionality of links between concepts.[19]
- Students may find it easiest to work on paper while they learn how to construct a map.

Face-to-Face Sessions

- Facilitate the first face-to-face session in any classroom with a large whiteboard. Large sticky notes are helpful to facilitate collaborative concept mapping.
- Facilitate the second face-to-face session in a computer lab so that students may practice searching for materials.

Learning Outcomes and Learning Activities

Learning Outcomes

1. Students will map their approach to research in order to identify important steps or stages of an academic research process (Session One).
2. Students will illustrate the connections between components of an academic research process in order to model an iterative, rather than linear, process (Session One).
3. Students will describe how information sources encountered at the beginning of their research process help them refine their topics or questions (Session Two).

Learning outcomes one and two are essential to expose and explore students' existing mental models, while learning outcome three is an optional opportunity to reinforce useful elements of an iterative process during the early stages of research.

Learning Activities

1. Pre-Session One: Research Map Activity *(LO1, 30–45 minutes homework, essential)*
    - Before the first face-to-face session, students review an online module to learn how to create a concept map that depicts their view of the research process. Training is an essential first step to any concept map activity,[20] and limited contact time with learners makes concept maps difficult to complete during traditional library instruction.[21] To solve this problem, learners create their concept map as part of the first pre-session online learning module.
    - Within the module, students review resources that demonstrate the steps to create a concept map.[22] Resources should illustrate how to label links between concepts; these labels

distinguish concept maps from "mind maps"[23] and require students to articulate the relationships among various components of the research process.
- Next, students draw a concept map depicting their view of the research process, based on the following assignment prompt:

> Now that you know how to create a concept map, use those skills to draw a map of what you think the process looks like for writing a college-level research paper. Remember to follow the principles laid out in the concept mapping resources. You should brainstorm a list of stages, activities, and information resources, arrange these concepts onto your map, draw linkages between related concepts, and label the links. Draw your final map on a sheet of paper and bring it with you to your first library instruction session.

2. Session One: Research Map In-Class Instruction *(LO1-2, 25–30 minutes, essential)*
    - Conduct the first face-to-face session before students begin their research projects, and work with students to create a collaborative class concept map of the research process. This process should help students analyze their own approach to research and discover new connections among components of an iterative research process. Students begin revising their mental models when they compare individual concept maps to those of their peers or the instructor.[24]
    - First, students compare their individual "Writing a Research Paper" concept maps with a partner.
        - ▷ Ask students to identify overlapping or essential concepts (at least three to five concepts) and linkages.
        - ▷ Distribute slips of paper or large sticky notes; students should write one essential concept on each piece of paper.
    - On a large whiteboard, begin the collaborative class map by placing key beginning (i.e., reading the assignment) and ending (i.e., submitting the assignment) points of the research process at opposite ends of the board.

- ▷ Students place their essential concepts onto the class map. Using the sticky notes makes it easy for students to rearrange concepts as necessary.
- ▷ Finally, help students finish the map by leading a discussion to add key missing stages or resources, organize the map, and establish links among the concepts. Input from the librarian and the professor models an expert's approach to research.
- ▷ Take a picture of the map to post to the course LMS site.
- ▷ Collect individual maps for assessment.

- Ideally, the class concept map includes:
  - ▷ multiple in-going and out-going links between research and writing tasks, indicating an iterative process;
  - ▷ early phases of the research process depicted as an opportunity to ask and answer questions; and
  - ▷ linkages within the map that demonstrate a recursive relationship between information sources and the research topic or question.

3. Pre-Session Two: Background Searching *(10–15 minutes homework, essential)*
   - A successful conceptual change learning environment reinforces how a new mental model is useful,[25] and the second pre-activity uses the uncertainty of topic selection as motivation for students to review their approach. Focusing on how an iterative view of the research process creates space for initial sources to refine or change a topic should help students discover the relationship between the information they find and their ultimate research directions.
     - ▷ Students watch a video that demonstrates how initial searches help to narrow or redefine a research topic.[26]
     - ▷ Students review the collaborative class concept map from Session One and describe the relationship between the research process, information sources, and topic selection, based on the following assignment prompt:

> Based on the video and our class research process map, how do you think choosing a topic fits into your research process? How can background research help you select or improve your topic?

4. Session Two: Background Searching In-Class Instruction *(LO3, 50–75 minutes, essential)*
   - This session starts with an everyday information-seeking task that can be used as an analogy to academic research. The analogy should be used to connect students' everyday information strategies to beginning phases of an iterative research process. For example, if your campus has a culture of study abroad participation, you may consider the following:

> Pretend the University will pay for you to study anywhere in the world for one semester. What steps would you follow to plan your semester abroad? Consider factors like which country and city you would visit, where you would study, how you would decide to travel, and anything else you think is important.

   - Students first discuss this prompt with a partner (five to seven minutes), followed by a full-class discussion (ten minutes).
   - Write down and organize students' overarching themes or steps in the process on a whiteboard and point out connections to the collaborative research process map.
     - ▷ For example, students may describe selecting a specific geographic location for study before narrowing to a specific university based on academic programs. This process is analogous to selecting a general research topic based on personal experience while narrowing one's focus based on preliminary results.
   - Whichever analogy you choose should "bridge" students' naïve conceptions of the research process to a more complex approach.[27]
   - Use direct instruction to introduce background research as an opportunity to narrow or clarify research topics, understand new directions, identify scholarly vocabulary, or find links and citations to other sources.
   - Demonstrate search tips useful for using the library's academic databases to find background information (ten to fifteen minutes).

- Using the rest of the class time and finishing as homework, students search for two background sources and use a worksheet to describe what they learn from each source (see Appendix 3A: "Sample Worksheet Questions for Background Searching").
    - ▷ Tailor the worksheet to the library's resources, guiding students to the best databases to use for background information.
- In the worksheet, students pose new questions about their topic based on the two sources. Students should discover how they could refine their research topics or questions due to early exploration.
- Emphasizing that professors expect this process to occur should ease fears about topic selection and tap into students' drive to fulfill their professor's expectations.
- Collect student worksheets for assessment.

5. End of the Semester
    - Due to the short-term nature of course-embedded library instruction, conceptual change is difficult to detect immediately after class. More likely, this instruction coupled with experience working through the research process influences students' long-term conceptual change.
    - At the end of the semester, students once again complete a concept map of their research process using resources from the first pre-session module.
    - Students complete the map as homework and submit it to the librarian for assessment.

Assessment

Summative assessment for learning outcomes one and two uses individual concept maps completed before instruction sessions, the maps completed at the end of the semester, and the worksheet from session two. Concept maps are particularly useful for pre- and post-instruction assessment because they can detect changes in students' mental models.[28]

Assessing Learning Outcome One

Count the number of concepts in each student's map as well as the number of concepts added (from the first to the second map).[29] Successful students should list more concepts in the second concept map, which demonstrates a more complex understanding of the research process.

Assessing Learning Outcome Two

Evaluate each student concept map for the number of links and map complexity (the ratio of links to concepts).[30] Successful students will draw a more complex, iterative approach to research, and their second map should include more links and higher complexity scores.

Assessing Learning Outcome Three

The final question from students' second instruction session worksheet is a summative assessment of how initial sources influence topic refinement or research direction. This question asks students to describe how their specific topic changes after initial searching. Successful students should articulate what they learned from background research and how they refined their topic.

To understand whether students shifted their mental models to account for a recursive relationship between research topics and information sources, examine the final concept maps to see if students include both outgoing and incoming links between topics and sources.

Appendix 3A

Sample Worksheet Questions for Background Searching

Think About Your Topic

1. What is one topic you're considering researching for your class project?
2. What would you like to learn about this topic before you finalize your decision?

Find Background Information—Using the skills we learned in class, find two sources you can use to learn more about your research topic. At least one source must come from the library's resources (either electronic or print). Answer the questions below to evaluate your source.

SOURCE 1

- What type of source is this (e.g., encyclopedia entry, book, blog, Wikipedia page, etc.)?
- What is the title of the source?
- Who is/are the author(s)?
- What does this source help you learn about your topic? Try to discuss 2–3 new ideas.
- What is at least one new question you have about your topic?

SOURCE 2

- What type of source is this (e.g., encyclopedia entry, book, blog, Wikipedia page, etc.)?
- What is the title of the source?
- Who is/are the author(s)?
- What does this source help you learn about your topic? Try to discuss 2–3 new ideas.
- What is at least one new question you have about your topic?

Bring it all Together: Your Research Direction—Use what you've learned from these two sources to focus your research direction.

3. Based on what you've read so far, how would you like to revise or change your research topic? Make sure to explain how the sources you found helped you think about your initial research idea.

Notes

1. Association of College and Research Libraries, *Framework for Information Literacy for Higher Education*," February 2, 2015, http://www.ala.org/acrl/sites/ala.org.acrl/files/content/issues/infolit/Framework_ILHE.pdf.
2. Ibid, 7.
3. M. J. Braun and Sarah Prineas, "First-year Composition as an Introduction to Academic Discourse," in *Strategies for Teaching First-Year Composition*, ed. Duane Roen, et al. (Urbana: National Council for Teachers of English, 2002), 574–75, http://files.eric.ed.gov/fulltext/ED459476.pdf; Wendy Holliday and Qin Li, "Understanding the Millennials: Updating Our Knowledge About Students," *Reference Services Review* 32, no. 4 (2004): 363–64, https://www.emeraldinsight.com/doi/full/10.1108/00907320410569707.
4. Sonia Bodi, "How Do We Bridge the Gap Between What We Teach and What They Do? Some Thoughts on the Place of Questions in the Process of Research," *The Journal of Academic Librarianship* 28, no. 3 (2002): 111, doi: 10.1016/S0099-1333(01)00302-0; Firouzeh Logan and Elizabeth Pickard, "First-Generation College Students: A Sketch of Their Research Process," in *College Libraries and Student Culture: What We Know*, ed. Lynda M. Duke and Andrew D. Asher (Chicago: American Library Association, 2012), 116–18, Ebrary Academic Complete; Whitney M. Olsen and Anne R. Diekema, "'I Just Wikipedia It': Information Behavior of First-Year Writing Students," *Proceedings of the Association for Information Science and Technology* 49, no. 1 (2012): 5, doi: 10.1002/meet.14504901176.
5. Melissa Gross and Don Latham, "Undergraduate Perceptions of Information Literacy: Defining, Attaining, and Self-Assessing Skills," *College & Research Libraries* 70, no. 4 (2009): 342, doi: 10.5860/crl.70.4.336; Barbara Valentine, "The Legitimate Effort in Research Papers: Student Commitment Versus Faculty Expectations," *The Journal of Academic Librarianship* 27, no. 2 (2001): 108, doi: 10.1016/S0099-1333(00)00182-8.
6. Susan Carey, "Knowledge Acquisition: Enrichment or Conceptual Change," in *Concepts: Core Readings*, ed. Eric Margolis and Stephan Laurence (Cambridge: MIT Press, 1999), 460.
7. Ibid, 461.
8. Jan Meyer and Ray Land, "Threshold Concepts and Troublesome Knowledge: Linkages to Ways to Thinking and Practising Within the Disciplines," *ETL Project Occasional Report 4, Enhancing Teaching-Learning Environments in Undergraduate Course Project*, http://www.etl.tla.ed.ac.uk/docs/ETLreport4.pdf.
9. Peter Davies and Jean Mangan, "Threshold Concepts and the Integration of Understanding in Economics," *Studies in Higher Education* 32, no. 6 (2007): 715, doi:10.1080/03075070701685148; Max Scheja and Anna Bonnevier, "Conceptualising Students' Experiences of Understanding in Medicine," *Psychology: The Journal of Hellenic Psychological Society* 17, no. 3 (2010): 243–58.
10. George Posner et al., "Accommodation of a Scientific Conception: Toward a Theory of Conceptual Change," *Science Education* 66, no. 2 (1982), 214.
11. Kaarina Merenluoto and Erno Lehtinen, "Number Concept and Conceptual Change: Towards a Systematic Model of the Processes of Change," *Learning and Instruction* 14 (2004), 523–26, doi: 10.1016/j.learninstruc.2004.06.016.
12. George Posner et al., "Accommodation of a Scientific Conception," 214.
13. Esther S. Grassian and Joan R. Kaplowitz, "Library Anxiety, Mental Models, and Conceptual Change," in *Information Literacy Instruction: Theory and Practice*, 2nd ed. (New York: Neal-Shuman Publisher, 2009): 73–83.
14. David Jonassen, Johannes Strobel, and Joshua Gottdenker, "Model Building for Conceptual Change," *Interactive Learning Environments* 13, no 1–2 (2005): 19, doi: 10.1080/10494820500173292.
15. Naomi R. Sutherland and C. M. Winters, "The A, B. Z's of Bibliographic Instruction: Using Real-Life Analogies to Foster Understanding," *Reference Librarian* 35, no. 73 (2001): 294, doi: 10.1300/J120v35n73_06.

16. Marcus Lee Johnson and Gale M. Sinatra, "Use of Task-Value Instructional Inductions," *Contemporary Educational Psychology* 38 (2013): 59. doi: 10.1016/j.cedpsych.2012.09.003.
17. Alison J. Head and Michael B. Eisenberg, "Truth Be Told: How College Students Evaluate and Use Information in the Digital Age," *Project Information Literacy Progress Report* (2010): 21, 33, http://www.projectinfolit.org/uploads/2/7/5/4/27541717/pil_fall2010_survey_fullreport1.pdf; Logan and Pickard, "First-generation College Students," 113; Hannah Gascho Rempel, Stefanie Buck, and Anne-Marie Deitering, "Examining Student Research Choices and Processes in a Disintermediated Search Environment," *portal: Libraries and the Academy* 13, no. 4 (2012), 378, doi: 10.1353/pla.2013.0036.
18. Ethelene Whitmire, "Epistemological Beliefs and the Information-Seeking Behavior of Undergraduates," *Library and Information Science Research* 25, no. 2, (2003): 127–42, doi: 10.1016/S0740-8188(03)00003-3.
19. For example, Cmap Cloud, https://cmapcloud.ihmc.us/.
20. Maria Pinto, Anne-Vinciane Doucet, and Andrés Fernández-Ramos, "Measuring Students' Information Skills Through Concept Mapping," *Journal of Information Science* 36, no 4 (2010): 467, doi:10.1177/0165551510369633.
21. Heidi Gauder and Fred Jenkins, "Engaging Undergraduates in Discipline-based Research," *Reference Services Review* 40, no. 2 (2012); 291, doi: 10.1108/00907321211228327; Carolyn J. Radcliff et al., "Concept Maps," in *A Practical Guide to Information Literacy Assessment for Academic Librarians* (Westport: Libraries Unlimited, 2007): 107.
22. For example, ITS Training Services, "Concept Maps," *iStudy for Success! Online Learning Tutorials for Essential College Skills*, last modified November 4, 2014, http://tutorials.istudy.psu.edu/conceptmaps/index.html; "Concept Mapping," YouTube video, 1:43, posted by "uPittBradford," July 25, 2012, https://youtu.be/8uoZpTYmrmo; or "Concept Maps—A Visual Study Tool," YouTube video, 3:25, posted by "nooluoit," August 30, 2011, https://youtu.be/vuBLI6ijHHg.
23. April Colosimo and Megan Fitzgibbons, "Teaching, Designing, and Organizing: Concept Mapping for Librarians," *Partnership: The Canadian Journal of Library & Information Practice & Research* 7, no. 1 (2012): 2, doi: 10.21083/partnership.v7i1.1800.
24. Jonassen, Strobel, and Gottdenker, "Model Building for Conceptual Change," 23.
25. Johnson and Sinatra, "Use of Task-Value Instructional Inductions," 59–60.
26. For example, Burke et al., "Picking Your Topic is Research," *North Carolina State University*, last modified August 2013, *Libraries*, http://lib.ncsu.edu/tutorials/picking_topic/.
27. Sutherland and Winters, "The A, B, Z's of Bibliographic Instruction," 294.
28. Colosimo and Fitzgibbons, "Teaching, Designing, and Organizing," 11; Radcliff et al., "Concept Mapping," 107.
29. Sally Sue Richmond, Joanna F. Defranco, and Kathryn Jablokow, "A Set of Guidelines for the Consistent Assessment of Concept Maps," *International Journal of Engineering Education* 30, no. 5 (2014): 1077–78.
30. Ibid, 1077–81.

Bibliography

Association of College and Research Libraries. *Framework for Information Literacy for Higher Education*. February 2, 2015. http://www.ala.org/acrl/standards/ilframework.

Bodi, Sonia. "How Do We Bridge the Gap Between What We Teach and What They Do? Some Thoughts on the Place of Questions in the Process of Research." *The Journal of Academic Librarianship* 28, no. 3 (2002): 109–14. doi: 10.1016/S0099-1333(01)00302-0.

Braun, M. J., and Sarah Prineas. "First-Year Composition as an Introduction to Academic Discourse." In *Strategies for Teaching First-Year Composition*, edited by Duane Roen, et al., 570–82. Urbana: National Council of Teachers of English. 2002. http://files.eric.ed.gov/fulltext/ED459476.pdf.

Burke, Anne, Kim Duckett, Daria Dorafshar, Mara Mathews, Jason Evans Groth, Andreas Orphanides, Sarah Craig, and Jennifer Garret. "Picking Your Topic is Research." North Carolina State University Libraries. Last modified August 2013. http://www.lib.ncsu.edu/tutorials/picking_topic/.

Carey, Susan. "Knowledge Acquisition: Enrichment or Conceptual Change." In *Concepts: Core Readings*, edited by Eric Margolis and Stephen Laurence, 459–87. Cambridge: MIT Press, 1999.

Colosimo, April, and Megan Fitzgibbons. "Teaching, Designing, and Organizing: Concept Mapping for Librarians." *Partnership: The Canadian Journal of Library & Information Practice & Research* 7, no. 1 (2012): 1–15. doi: 10.21083/partnership.v7i1.1800.

"Concept Mapping." YouTube video, 1:43. Posted by "uPittBradford," July 25, 2012. https://youtu.be/8uoZpTYmrmo.

"Concept Maps—A Visual Study Tool." YouTube video, 3:25. Posted by "nooluoit," August 30, 2011. https://youtu.be/vuBLI6ijHHg.

Davies, Peter, and Jean Mangan. "Threshold Concepts and the Integration of Understanding in Economics." *Studies in Higher Education* 32, no. 6 (2007): 711–26. doi: 10.1080/03075070701685148.

Gauder, Heidi, and Fred Jenkins. "Engaging Undergraduates in Discipline-based Research." *Reference Services Review* 40, no. 2 (2012): 277–94. doi: 10.1108/00907321211228327.

Grassian, Esther S., and Joan R. Kaplowitz. "Library Anxiety, Mental Models, and Conceptual Change." In *Information Literacy Instruction: Theory and Practice*, 2nd ed., 65–84. New York: Neal-Schuman Publishers, 2009.

Gross, Melissa and Don Latham. "Undergraduate Perceptions of Information Literacy: Defining, Attaining, and Self-Assessing Skills." *College & Research Libraries* 70, no. 4 (2009): 336–50. doi: 10.5860/crl.70.4.336.

Head, Alison J., and Michael B. Eisenberg. "Truth Be Told: How College Students Evaluate and Use Information in the Digital Age." Project Information Literacy, November 1, 2010. http://www.projectinfolit.org/uploads/2/7/5/4/27541717/pil_fall2010_survey_fullreport1.pdf.

Holliday, Wendy, and Qin Li. "Understanding the Millennials: Updating Our Knowledge About Students." *Reference Services Review* 32, no. 4 (2004): 356–66. doi: 10.1108/00907320410569707.

ITS Training Services. "Concept Maps." iStudy for Success! Online Learning Tutorials for Essential College Skills. Last modified November 4, 2014. http://tutorials.istudy.psu.edu/conceptmaps/index.html.

Johnson, Marcus Lee, and Gale M. Sinatra. "Use of Task-Value Instructional Inductions for Facilitating Engagement and Conceptual Change." *Contemporary Educational Psychology* 38 (2013): 51–63. doi: 10.1016/j.cedpsych.2012.09.003.

Jonassen, David, Johannes Strobel, and Joshua Gottdenker. "Model Building for Conceptual Change." *Interactive Learning Environments* 13, no. 1-2 (2005): 15–37. doi: 10.1080/10494820500173292.

Logan, Firouzeh, and Elizabeth Pickard. "First-generation College Students: A Sketch of Their Research Process." In *College Libraries and Student Culture: What We Know Now*, edited by Lynda M. Duke and Andrew D. Asher, 109–25. Chicago: American Library Association, 2012. Ebrary Academic Complete.

Merenluoto, Kaarina, and Erno Lehtinen. "Number Concept and Conceptual Change: Towards a Systemic Model of the Processes of Change." *Learning and Instruction* 14 (2004): 519–34. doi: 10.1016/j.learninstruc.2004.06.016.

Meyer, Jan, and Ray Land. "Threshold Concepts and Troublesome Knowledge: Linkages to Ways of Thinking and Practising Within the Disciplines," *ETL Project Occasional Report 4, Enhancing Teaching-Learning Environments in Undergraduate Courses Project*, May 2003. http://www.etl.tla.ed.ac.uk/docs/ETLreport4.pdf.

Olsen, M. Whitney, and Anne R. Diekema. "'I Just Wikipedia It': Information Behavior of First-Year Writing Students." *Proceedings of the Association for Information Science and Technology* 49, no. 1 (2012): 1–11. doi: 10.1002/meet.14504901176.

Pinto, Maria, Anne-Vinciane Doucet, and Andrés Fernández-Ramos. "Measuring Students' Information Skills Through Concept Mapping." *Journal of Information Science* 36, no. 4 (2010): 464–80. doi: 10.1177/0165551510369633.

Posner, George J., Kenneth A. Strike, Peter W. Hewson, and William A. Gertzog. "Accommodation of a Scientific Conception: Toward a Theory of Conceptual Change." *Science Education* 66, no. 2 (1982): 211–27.

Radcliff, Carolyn J., Mary Lee Jensen, Joseph A. Salem Jr., Kenneth J. Burhanna, and Julie A. Gedeon. "Concept Maps," in *A Practical Guide to Information Literacy Assessment for Academic Librarians*, 106–14. Westport: Libraries Unlimited, 2007.

Rempel, Hannah Gascho, Stefanie Buck, and Anne-Marie Deitering. "Examining Student Research Choices and Processes in a Disintermediated Searching Environment." *portal: Libraries and the Academy* 13, no. 4 (2013): 363–84. doi: 10.1353/pla.2013.0036.

Richmond, Sally Sue, Joanna F. Defranco, and Kathryn Jablokow. "A Set of Guidelines for the Consistent Assessment of Concept Maps." *International Journal of Engineering Education* 30, no. 5 (2014): 1072–82. http://www.ijee.ie/contents/c300514.html.

Scheja, Max, and Anna Bonnevier. "Conceptualising Students' Experiences of Understanding in Medicine." *Psychology: The Journal of the Hellenic Psychological Society* 17, no. 3 (2010): 243–58.

Sutherland, Naomi R., and C.M. Winters. "The A, B, Z's of Bibliographic Instruction: Using Real-Life Analogies to Foster Understanding." *Reference Librarian* 35, no. 73 (2001): 293–308. doi: 10.1300/J120v35n73_06.

Valentine, Barbara. "The Legitimate Effort in Research Papers: Student Commitment Versus Faculty Expectations." *The Journal of Academic Librarianship* 27, no. 2 (2001): 107–15. doi: 10.1016/S0099-1333(00)00182-8.

Whitmire, Ethelene. "Epistemological Beliefs and the Information-Seeking Behavior of Undergraduates." *Library and Information Science Research* 25, no. 2 (2003), 127–42. doi: 10.1016/S0740-8188(03)00003-3.

CHAPTER 4

TOPIC Generation and Teaching Research as Inquiry

Katie Hassman
Undergraduate Engagement Librarian
University of Iowa

Benjamin Hassman
Lecturer, Rhetoric
University of Iowa

ACRL Information Literacy Frame: Research as Inquiry
Discipline: Arts & Humanities
Subject: Rhetoric; First-Year Writing; Inquiry
Learning Theory: Academic Literacies
Special Populations: First-Year Students; Undergraduate Students

Developing research questions and topics remains one of the more challenging steps for undergraduate students completing research projects and assignments.[1,2] Yet the process of developing a research topic is often made invisible through popular, open-ended assignment prompts, like "choose a topic that interests you" or "ask a question you're passionate about exploring." Without support and instruction, we can leave students guessing about what a good research topic or question looks like, shifting the responsibility of identifying curiosities and refining topics squarely onto the student.[3,4]

ACRL Information Literacy Frame: Research as Inquiry

The Research as Inquiry frame from the ACRL Framework describes knowledge practices and dispositions particularly relevant to teaching stu dents how to develop research questions and topics. As an example, the frame focuses on

- determining the scope of investigation;
- managing complex topics and developing sub-questions to limit scope;
- meaningfully organizing information; and
- valuing curiosity and persistence in developing research projects and questions.[5]

While these practices and dispositions can inform a process-based approach to helping students develop skills and ideas relevant to developing research topics, the role of affect, emotion, and contextual norms is largely absent from these descriptions. Noting this absence is particularly important.

Learning Theory: Academic Literacies

As academics, we know the thrill that can come from pursuing a research topic or question that fascinates or compels us. As instructors, we often want to share this type of experience with our students: we want to show them the beauty and excitement of impassioned inquiry. And our students are often excited about this opportunity as well. Coming from high school contexts, where prescriptive paper topics and assignment prompts are typical, being provided the space and opportunity to pursue one's own interest can be particularly empowering and exciting for new undergraduate students.[6]

We also know that the research process can be incredibly emotional[7] and that learning to complete coursework often requires new sets of skills along with a nuanced understanding of the contextual and social norms that accompany college-level work.[8,9] Learning theories can help us better understand these dimensions. One theory in particular, academic literacies, helps focus attention on the nuanced and situated nature of research by describing the often "deep affective and ideological conflicts" students experience as they move into meaning-making practices in higher educational contexts.[10] Academic literacies perspectives value student identities and meanings, understanding that power relations and social norms and expectations are entangled with the seemingly practical work of the research process.[11,12] A first-year student new to higher education, for example, may be excited to be offered the chance to write a paper or develop a speech on a topic of their own choosing yet be met with frustration when they realize that what they are excited about is too broad or too narrow for their project. Emotionally connected to the topic, they may resist suggestions to explore alternative perspectives or to simplify their focus as they may feel—often rightly so—that they are experts on their topics. Locating alternative perspectives may seem to only muddy the waters and make summarizing and synthesizing perspectives especially challenging for students maintaining simplistic assumptions of objectivity (often a holdover from previous dichotomous understandings of bias). In this way, the seemingly practical activity of choosing a topic becomes an epistemological and affective issue that needs to be expressed and understood. And while we should not foist the unpacking of all research issues on a single, semester-length course, we can provide a space to channel first-year students' excitement and perceived freedom into beginning the process.

While the Research as Inquiry framework describes research as being the product of "collaborative effort" and the process as including "points of disagreement" and "dialogue," we need to further explore ways of incorporating these and other social and affective facets into our library instruction practice. We do our students a disservice if we do not show them how to channel their ideas and excitement, if we do not provide encouragement that can help them trust their ideas as valid and respected in academic contexts. We do our students a disservice if we do not let them know that the ups and downs of research, the conversations with peers, the dialogue with instructors is not intended to be—nor should it—be a neutral process; it is and can be frustrating on a practical level but also on a personal level. We do our students a disservice if we are not upfront about the expectations we have about them and how these are part of a larger social and institutional power structure that determines what is considered "academic work." In short, we do our students a disservice if we do not take their excitement as honest and provide a structured opportunity to support them as they explore this excitement in an honest yet practical way.

Talking of Projects Inspires Curiosity: TOPIC Teaching Module

TOPIC is a process-based teaching module that includes activities, assignments, and an informal, low-stakes workshop that supports the development of research questions and topics. TOPIC draws on the theory of academic literacies to make the affective practice and institutional norms of developing a research topic visible. The TOPIC workshop[13] is designed to provide a space and the necessary support to help students reflect on the experience of these multiple dimensions of developing research questions as undergraduate students. The workshop environment is intentionally social with activities that help draw explicit connections among the social environments created during the workshop and the social and institutional environment in which students now find themselves doing work. The TOPIC module is focused to meet learning objectives drawn from both the Research as Inquiry frame and the academic literacies model. For more on this, see the Assessment section.

While portions of the TOPIC module are designed to be co-taught, instructors of undergraduate courses could easily lead the co-taught portions, freeing up time for the librarian to spend more time on search techniques or other general information literacy instruction that can complement the activity/assignment research parameters.

Lesson Plan

Learner Analysis

- The TOPIC module is designed to supplement and support instruction in an undergraduate-level course with a research assignment component. This module works particularly well with first-year students as it takes a process approach to teaching research and provides opportunities for students to reflect on and ask questions about college-level research assignment requirements in informal, low-stakes contexts.
- This activity was developed in collaboration with faculty and instructors teaching a required undergraduate general education course teaching critical thinking, reading, research, writing, listening, and speaking skills. The curriculum for the course is

built on the understanding of the public importance of diverse responses to controversial topics and a goal of many courses is to help students move beyond dichotomous notions of arguments and topics. Given this context, the workshop is particularly well-suited for classes and coursework seeking to help students move beyond simple understandings of topics by providing active-learning activities that ask students to identify multiple viewpoints and missing perspectives.
- While this activity works well in first-year courses with research/inquiry components, TOPIC can also be framed to work in upper-level and honors-level coursework, as well as it is designed as a peer-review context that mimics professional research experiences.

Limitations

- While it can be challenging to teach research process to students with varying degrees of previous research experience, the workshop is built to leverage these differences through peer-feedback and support activities.

Opportunities

- Providing time for questions throughout the workshop prompts student reflection on learning and provides time for students to clarify workshop and/or assignment goals and the chance to ask clarifying questions about the research process more generally. Given the community-building that often happens as a result of collaborative activities like those included in this workshop, students may feel comfortable asking more difficult questions about the nature of academic research assignments. For example, during a session run by the authors, students asked clarifying questions, like:
    - ▷ How do I ensure that I adequately answer my research question?
    - ▷ How specific should a question be at this point?
    - ▷ How do you pick a side to a topic when there are so many different sides to the topic?
    - ▷ How do you objectively report on the topic without being bias?

These questions prompted conversation about academic norms and expectations. We asked students to reflect on and share their previous experience and understanding of concepts like bias, so the conversation was grounded in helping students understand the differences between expectations in higher education and high school contexts, a conscious application of the academic literacies model.

Orienting Context and Prerequisites

- Students should have received course assignment requirements.
- Students should have completed the TOPIC Pre-Workshop Assignment prior to attending the TOPIC Workshop.

TOPIC Pre-Workshop Assignment

In preparation for the workshop, students are asked to reflect on their own understanding of research and research topics and identify a broad research topic of interest to them. After identifying the topic, students must brainstorm related keywords. Appendix 4A contains the worksheets students should complete and bring with them to the workshop.

Instructional Context

The following describes the TOPIC Workshop activity:

Materials required:

- whiteboards or easel-size sticky notes or sticky notes or 8.5×11 sheets of paper
- writing utensils, dependent on the writing surface, one for each student
- clock or timer
- phone with a camera (optional)
- TOPIC Brainstorm & Crowdsource Workshop Handouts, one for each student
- students need to bring completed TOPIC Pre-Workshop Assignment to the workshop

It is optimal to have a room large enough for all students to move around in and enough whiteboards for each student to have their own space to write questions. If whiteboards are not available but there is enough space in the room, easel-size Post-its or regular size Post-it Notes can be used to record student questions. If whiteboards are not available or there are learners with mobility impairments, the activity can be completed with 8.5×11 sheets of paper. In this scenario, each student should have their own sheets of paper to be passed around the class. It is ideal to bring along enough writing utensils, whiteboard markers, pens, or pencils so that each student has their own. A clock or timer is required so the instructor can time the brainstorm rounds. We have found it helpful to take photos of brainstormed lists written on whiteboards or on sticky notes attached to the wall after the workshop to share with the larger class. If 8.5×11 sheets of paper are used, collect these from students to scan and share with the class for subsequent discussion.

Prior to students' arrival, complete the following:

- Set up the classroom in stations, one per student. At each station place: a Post-it sheet or a stack of Post-it Notes or two to three pieces of 8.5×11-inch paper, along with appropriate writing utensils. If you have whiteboard space available, place a marker at each station.
- Plan workshop timing. The workshop is built around multiple "crowdsource" rounds, where students will provide feedback to peers and brainstorm additional research questions related to a student's broad topics. See the table below in the Instructional Objectives and Learning Activities Section.

We have found it helpful in the run-up to the assignment to talk rather explicitly about research questions, thesis statements, and the inherent difficulty in writing an appropriate question within a topic that students may not know much about. In many cases, their cursory understanding of the traditional "controversy" essay makes their work more difficult by giving things the appearance of stark dichotomy (and thereby simplicity) when really the research space is a messy place with opaque borders. In this light, it is helpful to work through concrete examples with students. This can take many forms, including on-campus issues from the frivolous (e.g., the best dormitory) to the serious (e.g., why college is still worth the investment), or real-world issues (like worry about the Ebola outbreak). Working through concrete examples in class prior to the TOPIC Workshop helps students see how an initial question or thesis gets sharper through rounds of revisions and research.

Learning Outcomes and Activities

Learning Outcomes

1. Students formulate questions and synthesize ideas.
2. Students critically evaluate questions, formulate questions, and identify gaps.
3. Students organize and conceptualize information to identify possible gaps or missing perspectives.
4. Students determine an appropriate and meaningful scope of investigation.
5. Students describe justifications and meaning of chosen research questions.
6. Students reflect on the social nature of scholarship in the academy.

Learning Activities

1. Topic and Question Brainstorming *(LO1, 5 minutes, essential)*
    - Students write their broad topic on the whiteboard. Then students use their keyword brainstorm from the Pre-Workshop Assignment (Appendix 4A) and the "Research Lenses" (Appendix 4C) table in the TOPIC Workshop Handout (Appendix 4B) to brainstorm and record as many possible research questions about their broad topic as they can come up with.
        - ▷ Note: It is ideal if students develop questions for a particular assignment.
2. Crowdsourced Rounds *(LO2, 3 minutes per round, essential)*
    - Students rotate one station to the right or left or hand their papers to the person next to them. Then students use the "Research Lenses" chart (Appendix 4C) to add questions to their classmate's existing brainstormed list. In addition to adding questions, students should also be encouraged to write clarifying questions or notes about existing questions, as well as a star or otherwise mark questions they feel are particularly well written or compelling.
        - ▷ Note: It is ideal for each student to receive at least three rounds of feedback. Saturation and boredom tend to set in around round five or six.
3. Review and Organize Rounds *(LO3, 5–7 minutes, essential)*

- Students return to their original station and read through the questions developed about their topic. During this round, students organize questions into categories based on the perspectives the questions represent. Students using sticky notes can move notes around to create clusters. Students writing on the whiteboard or paper may write a list of the perspectives identified. Once complete, students should identify and write another list with perspectives not represented but of possible value to conversations about their broad topic. Students should then try to develop one or two questions from the missing perspectives.

4. Crowdsource Round *(LO2, 3 minutes per round; no more than 2 rounds, optional)*
   - Students rotate again, this time in the opposite direction and brainstorm additional questions framed from the "missing perspectives."
5. Quality Questions Round *(LO4, 5 minutes, essential)*
   - Students return to their original station and read through all the questions developed about their topic. During this round, students choose three to five questions they are interested in pursuing and feel meet the goals and parameters of their assignment. Students should record these questions on the provided TOPIC Brainstorm & Crowdsource Workshop handout (Appendix 4D).
6. Quality Questions Sharing *(LO5, 10–15 minutes, essential)*
   - Once students have completed their lists, volunteers should be asked to share their lists with the class (sharing only their top one or two questions), describing why they choose their questions and why they feel they would be good questions for their current assignment
7. Debrief *(LO6, 10 minutes, essential)*
   - Students return to desks or seats and respond to questions, like the following:
     - ▷ What did you think about this activity? How did you feel during the activity? What did you enjoy most? What did you enjoy the least? What was challenging?
     - ▷ Do you have questions about the assignment and how this activity relates?

8. Assessment *(LO6, 5–10 minutes, essential)*
    - Students complete Workshop Feedback Form (Appendix 4E), part of the TOPIC Workshop handout.

Assessment

Learning objectives can be assessed through a combination of: observation of workshop activities; a collection of a series of self-statements throughout the semester, leading up to and following the TOPIC Workshop; and authentic assessment of final student projects.

Observation

Observation should be conducted during the TOPIC workshop. The table below describes when observation can ideally be used to measure learning objectives during specific TOPIC Workshop activities.

Self-Statements

The series of self-statements are part of the TOPIC Workshop handouts, included at the end of this chapter. The self-statements should be collected at three times throughout the research process:

1. prior to beginning the research assignment (part of the TOPIC Pre-Workshop Assignment packet);
2. during the research process (after the completion of the TOPIC workshop, part of the TOPIC Workshop packet); and
3. after completing and handing in the research assignment (TOPIC Post-Workshop Assessment).

Authentic Assessment

Final student projects may be assessed to measure how students' final research question or topic met assignment parameters.

The table in Appendix 4F describes how data can be collected and learning outcomes measured throughout students' research process and during the associated TOPIC Workshop. Individual learning objectives are matched with associated data collection methods, measures, and the connecting theory and/or ACRL Frame.

Appendix 4A

Developing a Topic: Pre-Workshop Assignment

Identifying and developing a topic isn't easy. In fact, a good topic—one that is compelling, focused, and refined to fit assignment requirements—develops over the course of a research project or assignment. The following worksheet is designed to help you in this process.

1. Identify a broad topic.
2. Once you've chosen a broad topic to explore for your assignment, write your topic at the top of the Keyword Brainstorm worksheet attached.
3. Take 3–5 minutes and add as many words as you can about your topic under the broad categories provided on the Keyword Brainstorm worksheet. Try to come up with at least 2–3 words for each of the categories (Who, What, When, Why).
4. Use the words you just recorded as keywords to search online and in library resources to locate materials on your topic. As you search, record new terms you discover related to your topic. If you find a resource (an article, a blog post, a book, etc.) that is particularly relevant to your topic, take a moment and record the citation as you might want to return to that source later in your research.

Developing a Topic: Pre-Workshop Assignment

The following worksheet is designed to help you organize terms and ideas about your chosen topic.

1. Write your topic in the "Topic" space below.
2. Take 3–5 minutes and add as many words as you can about your topic under the broad categories provided (Who, What, When, Why). Try to come up with at least 2–3 words for each of the categories.
3. Using the words you just recorded, search one or more of the sources and tools provided in the Tools and Sources section above. As you search, try to find a few more terms that relate to your topic. As you come across more terms, record these below as well. If you find an information resource (an article, a blog post, a book, etc.) that is particularly relevant to your topic, take a moment and record the citation as you might want to return to that source later in your research.

Topic:

WHO	WHAT	WHEN	WHY

Developing a Topic: Pre-Workshop Assignment

Reflections

Please respond as honestly and as best you can to the following prompts.

1. Please describe how you expect to learn about developing a topic in this course.
2. What does a topic do? What is its purpose?
3. In your own words, define the term "topic."

Appendix 4B
Developing a Topic: TOPIC Workshop

Identifying and developing a topic isn't easy. In fact, a good topic—one that is compelling, focused, and refined to fit assignment requirements—often develops in fits and stages over the course of a research project or assignment. The following worksheet is an outline and guide for today's Topic Brainstorm and Crowdsource Workshop. This workshop is designed to help you along the path of developing your topics for your next assignment.

Materials required:

- Completed Keyword Brainstorm handout
- Willingness to learn new investigative methods that can: (1) help identify and explore multiple perspectives on a chosen topic; (2) help refine and narrow the focus of a chosen topic

1. Grab a marker or pen and write your research question or topic on the board or on the paper provided. If you are working at a whiteboard or other surface, make sure to bring along this handout along with your completed Keyword Brainstorm handout.
2. Your workshop leader/instructor will start a timer. For the duration of the timer, use the terms you recorded on your Keyword Brainstorm handout to develop research questions about your general topic. Each of your research questions should use one of the "lenses" provided below in the "Research Lenses" table.
3. Once the time has elapsed, your workshop leader/instructor will start another timer and begin the crowdsource round. At this time, move clockwise over to the next general topic. For the duration of the timer, add additional questions to your classmates' brainstorm list. Make sure that all your questions include one of the lenses provided below. If you get stuck and can't think of any additional questions, make notes, suggestions, or perhaps even put a star next to an existing question that you feel are particularly well written. Just make sure that your feedback is in some way constructive. ***Note: You will not use your keyword brainstorm handout during this round.***
4. Your instructor/workshop leader will prompt you to start and stop additional crowdsource rounds (step 4).

5. Review and Organize Round: Return to your original station. Review the questions listed under your topic. Do you see any themes emerging? Are there ways you could group the questions into categories around specific perspectives? For example, if your topic was "the cost of higher education," you may see questions written from the student perspective, an instructor perspective, or the perspective of a member of the public. If you are using a whiteboard and/or paper, make a list of the different perspectives. If you are using Post-it Notes, arrange the Post-its according to these perspectival categories. Once completed, write a list containing perspectives not represented but of possible value to conversations about your broad topic. Using the Research Lenses table, try to develop 1–2 new questions that are written from one of the "missing" perspectives.
6. Crowdsource Round II: Rotate, this time counterclockwise, to the next topic. For the duration of the timer, add additional questions that are written from one of the "missing" perspectives listed by your classmate. Make sure that all your questions include one of the lenses provided, below. If you get stuck and can't think of any additional questions, make notes, suggestions, or perhaps even put a star next to an existing question that you feel are particularly well written. Just make sure that your feedback is in some way constructive. ***Note: You will not use your keyword brainstorm handout during this round.***
7. Question Value and Quality: Return to your original station and read through all the questions developed about your topic. Choose three questions you are interested in pursuing for your current assignment. Why are you drawn to these questions? Are they a good fit for assignment parameters? Are you providing a glimpse into an often "missing" perspective? Feel free to combine questions if they are a good fit for your assignment. Record the questions you are interested in pursuing in the Research Question Form included in this document below. Tear the Research Question form off and hand it to your workshop leader/instructor before you leave.
8. Share: Volunteers share lists of three chosen research questions and describe why you chose questions and why they feel they would be a good fit for their current assignment.

Appendix 4C
Research Lenses

Which one? Informs perspectives or choices by synthesizing and comparing information about topic(s).	*Example: Which social media technology of the last 5–10 years has had the largest positive impact on personal relationships?*
How? Explores solutions or perspectives to particular problems or topics.	*Example: How should we solve the problem of rising student loan debt?*
What if? Explores solutions, perspectives, and options; can help form hypothesis.	*Example: What if the United States had national paid parental leave requirements, similar to that offered in countries like Denmark, Finland, and Iceland?*
Should? Explores ethical, moral, or practical ideas or solutions based on available information.	*Example: Should state money be used to fund school voucher or savings plan programs?*
Why? Explores connections and relationships that contribute to a topic or issue.	*Example: Why do students expect to get a good job after completing a college degree?*

The "Research Lenses" activity is adapted from Buffy Hamilton who writes at *The Unquiet Librarian* blog. The activity is drawn from the blog post accessible here: https://theunquietlibrarian.wordpress.com/2015/04/27/formulating-research-questions-with-birds-of-feather-collaboration-and-writable-surfaces/. The Research Lenses is based on work originally published by Riedling (2007) in *An Educator's Guide to Information Literacy*, p.22.

Appendix 4D
Developing A Topic: Handout Form

Name:

Research questions chosen:

In 1–3 sentences, describe one thing you learned today.

In 1–3 sentences, describe one thing you have a question about.

What does a topic do? What is its purpose?

In your own words, define the term “topic.”

Appendix 4E

Developing a Topic: Post-workshop reflections

Please respond as honestly and as best you can to the following prompts.

1. Please describe how you learned about developing a topic in this course.

2. What does a topic do? What is its purpose?

3. In your own words, define the term "topic."

4. Please rate the following on a scale from strongly disagree to strongly agree. Place an X in the box that best describes your feelings about each statement.

	Strongly disagree	**Disagree**	**Neither agree nor disagree**	**Agree**	**Strongly agree**
I am better at developing topics for course-related research after completing this class.					
Class activities helped me improve my abilities to develop research topics and questions.					
Class activities helped me improve my understanding of conducting research.					
Class activities helped me understand college-level research.					

Appendix 4F

Learning outcome	Data collection	Measure	Theory/ Frame
Students begin to see research and inquiry as an ongoing process that can be iterative, creative, frustrating, and exciting.	Self-statements	Measured as a change in student conceptualizations of research throughout the course of the semester. Indicative sample self-statements: *"Today I learned to look/think a little deeper into my thoughts.' 'There may be more questions to ask and they may compel us."*	Academic Literacies Research as Inquiry
Students develop a deeper understanding of developing research topics.	Self-statements	Measured as a change in student conceptualizations of developing a topic throughout the semester. Measured as nuanced reflections describing the process of developing a topic.	Academic Literacies Research as Inquiry
Students move beyond dichotomous conceptualizations of topics or controversies toward understanding multiple perspectives.	Observation of workshop activities Self-statements	Measured in students' practices identifying and defining multiple viewpoints related to their question/topic brainstorm activity. Indicative statements: *"I learned that there are many viewpoints that can be related to a particular topic." "I learned to dig deeper into the topic to come up with controversial questions. Everyone has a difference in opinion." "I learned one topic can create a lot of questions."*	Research as Inquiry
Students develop strategies for organizing and conceptualizing ideas, research questions, and topics.	Observation of workshop activities Self-statements	Measured in students' practices of organizing and describing the variety of perspective related to their topics.	Research as Inquiry

Students determine topics/questions appropriate to the scope of assignment or investigation.	Observation of workshop activities Authentic assessment of student final projects	Measured as students' practices of identifying and describing the best topic or question during TOPIC workshop. Success is measured as students' topics matching assignment parameters, could be assessed with a rubric.	Research as Inquiry
Students develop a deeper understanding of instructor and institutional standards and expectations of how to develop a research topic or question.	Observation of workshop activities; in particular, Debrief questions (see Instructional Objectives and Learning Activities Table, above) Self-statements	Measured as students' descriptions and conceptualizations of research standards and assignment requirements.	Academic Literacies

Notes

1. Alison J. Head, "How Freshmen Conduct Course Research Once They Enter College," *Project Information Literacy Research Report: "Learning the Ropes"* (2013), https://files.eric.ed.gov/fulltext/ED548262.pdf.
2. Alison J. Head and Michael B. Eisenberg, "Truth Be Told: How College Students Evaluate and Use Information in the Digital Age," *Project Information Literacy Report* (2010), http://www.projectinfolit.org/uploads/2/7/5/4/27541717/pil_fall2010_survey_fullreport1.pdf.
3. Anne-Marie Deitering and Hannah Gascho Rempel, "Sparking Curiosity: Librarians' Role," *In the Library With the Lead Pipe* 2017, http://www.inthelibrarywiththeleadpipe.org/2017/sparking-curiosity/.
4. Jean Donham, "College Ready—What Can We Learn from First-Year College Assignments? An Examination of Assignments in Iowa Colleges and Universities," *School Library Research* 17, (2014).
5. Association of College & Research Libraries, *Framework for Information Literacy for Higher Education*, 2016, http://www.ala.org/acrl/standards/ilframework#inquiry.
6. Head, "How Freshmen Conduct."
7. Carol C. Kuhlthau, "Inside the Search Process: Information Seeking from the User's Perspective," *Journal of the American Society for Information Science* 42, no. 5 (1991).
8. Mary R. Lea and Brian V. Street, "Student Writing in Higher Education: An Academic Literacies Approach," *Studies in Higher Education* 23, no. 2 (1998).
9. Mary R. Lea and Brian V. Street, "The 'Academic Literacies' Model: Theory and Applications," *Theory Into Practice* 45, no. 4 (2006).
10. Lea and Street, "Student Writing."
11. Ibid.

12. Lea and Street, "The 'Academic Literacies' model."
13. The workshop activities are modified from previous work done by Buffy Hamilton (B. Hamilton, "Moving from Our Mindmaps to More Focused Topics with Question Lenses and Musical Peer Review," *The Unquiet Librarian* (blog), October 27, 2014, https://theunquietlibrarian.wordpress.com/2014/10/27/moving-from-our-mindmaps-to-more-focused-topics-with-question-lenses-and-musical-peer-review/; Buffy Hamilton, "Formulating Research Questions with Birds of Feather Collaboration and Writable Surfaces," *The Unquiet Librarian* (blog), April 27 2015, https://theunquietlibrarian.wordpress.com/2015/04/27/formulating-research-questions-with-birds-of-feather-collaboration-and-writable-surfaces/; and adapted from Riedling (Ann Marlow Riedling, *An Educator's Guide to Information Literacy: What Every High School Senior Needs to Know* (Westport, CT: Libraries Unlimited, 2007).

Bibliography

Association of College & Research Libraries. *Framework for Information Literacy for Higher Education.* 2016. http://www.ala.org/acrl/standards/ilframework#inquiry.

Deitering, Anne-Marie, Hannah Gascho Rempel. "Sparking Curiosity: Librarians' Role." In the Library with the Lead Pipe. 2017. http://www.inthelibrarywiththeleadpipe.org/2017/sparking-curiosity/.

Donham, Jean. "College Ready—What Can We Learn from First-Year College Assignments? An Examination of Assignments in Iowa Colleges and Universities." *School Library Research* 17 (2014): 1–21.

Hamilton, Buffy. "Formulating Research Questions with Birds of Feather Collaboration and Writable Surfaces." *The Unquiet Librarian* (blog). April 27, 2015. https://theunquietlibrarian.wordpress.com/2015/04/27/formulating-research-questions-with-birds-of-feather-collaboration-and-writable-surfaces/.

________. "Moving from Our Mindmaps to More Focused Topics with Question Lenses and Musical Peer Review." *The Unquiet Librarian* (blog). October 27, 2014. https://theunquietlibrarian.wordpress.com/2014/10/27/moving-from-our-mindmaps-to-more-focused-topics-with-question-lenses-and-musical-peer-review/.

Head, Alison J. "How Freshmen Conduct Course Research Once They Enter College." *Project Information Literacy Research Report: "Learning the Ropes"* (2013). https://files.eric.ed.gov/fulltext/ED548262.pdf.

Head, Alison J., and Michael B. Eisenberg. "Truth Be Told: How College Students Evaluate and Use Information in the Digital Age." *Project Information Literacy Report* (2010). http://www.projectinfolit.org/uploads/2/7/5/4/27541717/pil_fall2010_survey_fullreport1.pdf.

Kuhlthau, Carol C. "Inside the Search Process: Information Seeking from the User's Perspective." *Journal of the American Society for Information Science* 42, no. 5 (1991): 361–71.

Lea, Mary R., and Brian V. Street. "Student Writing in Higher Education: An Academic Literacies Approach." *Studies in Higher Education* 23, no. 2, (1998): 157–73.

________. "The 'Academic Literacies' Model: Theory and Applications." *Theory into Practice* 45, no. 4 (2006): 368–77.

Riedling, Ann Marlow. *An Educator's Guide to Information Literacy: What Every High School Senior Needs to Know.* Westport, CT: Libraries Unlimited, 2007.

CHAPTER 5

Patch and PACT Writing:

Engaging Students with the ACRL Framework, Research as Inquiry

Kelly Diamond
Head, Libraries' Office of Curriculum and Instructional Support
West Virginia University

Laura Brady, Ph.D.
Professor of English & Eberly Professor of Outstanding Teaching
West Virginia University

ACRL Information Literacy Frame: Research as Inquiry
Discipline: Arts & Humanities
Subject: English Composition and Rhetoric
Instructional Strategies: Reflective Learning; Learning Transfer
Special Populations: Undergraduate Students; First-Year Students

It is the middle of the semester and you are teaching a composition course required of all students at your university. Your students have just submitted rough drafts of a researched argument. As you start to respond to the drafts, you look forward to seeing what Kara, a very strong student whose long-term plans include law school, has discovered. She has chosen to write about the pros and cons of concealed weapons on college campuses. It is a topic that has been in the news lately and it interests her for both legal and personal reasons. She has told you that she has had no problem finding material.

As you start to read her draft, there is something about the phrasing in the second paragraph that does not sound like Kara's voice. The details in the paragraph are not common knowledge, yet you are not seeing any quotation marks or author attribution in the body of the paper. As you skim to the last page of the draft, you see with some relief that Kara has at least included a brief list of works cited. So, what is going on?

You find yourself wondering if you are seeing an example of what Rebecca Moore Howard would call "patchwriting."[1] Howard uses the term to describe the practice of copying and pasting sentences from multiple sources and patching them into a new document—sometimes without changing more than a word or two. If Kara has, in fact, patched in someone else's words, you do not think this is a deliberate attempt to deceive. Kara is normally a skilled and confident writer. Given the quality of work you have come to expect from Kara, did she just get pressed for time? Or do you share responsibility for the problem? You quickly skim a few more drafts and realize that you may not have conveyed your lessons on research and source evaluation and integration as clearly as you had hoped.

You find yourself thinking of an article in the *Chronicle of Higher Education*, where Kurt Schick makes the case that "the uneven quality of information available online makes it more important for writers to know how to evaluate … their sources." He goes on to suggest that we as teachers "abandon our fixation on the form rather than the function of source attribution."[2] Schick is not abandoning the need for source attribution, but he is reminding you that the best way to promote academic integrity is to help your students select, summarize, and analyze their sources in ways that will help them present their own ideas effectively and ethically.

Fortunately—for you and your students—this assignment is still in draft form. There is time for Kara and her classmates to improve their writing. And there is time for you to revise your lesson. Since you are team teaching this research course with one of the university librarians, you set up a time when the two of you can talk through the research challenges (for both teachers and students), set some realistic expectations (for both teachers and students), and design an activity to help students understand and practice good habits.

Your colleague points out that our first-year writing students seem to find sources readily enough but are less able to synthesize and interpret what they find. That is the piece to focus on: research as inquiry. Together, you consider the skills that the students already possess. All sections of introductory composition at West Virginia University have been using four key questions to talk about writing challenges:[3]

1. Purpose: What exactly do I want to happen?
2. Audience: Who is reading, listening, or viewing?
3. Conventions: What is expected in this context?
4. Trouble spots: What could get in the way of my goals?

ACRL Information Literacy Frame: Research as Inquiry

Students remember the questions with the acronym PACT. Those questions, you decide, might also be used to help students understand the ACRL concept of Research as Inquiry. As the ACRL framework statement explains, "Research is iterative and depends upon asking increasingly complex or new questions whose answers in turn develop additional questions or lines of inquiry in any field."[4] Students are already familiar with PACT. Could they transfer their use of PACT questions for writing to guide their reading and evaluation of sources? After all, recent work on transfer suggests that language plays a large role in how writers connect old and new knowledge and practice.[5]

Instructional Strategies: Reflective Learning and Learning Transfer

You think a bit more about how transfer tends to work in education. Perkins and Salomon use the metaphors of hugging and bridging to describe two different types: "hugging" relies on a close connection where we take something we do almost automatically and adapt it to a similar situation;[6] "bridging," in contrast, requires a cognitive leap and asks us as learners to reflect back or project forward to make a connection. Perkins and Salomon advise instructors to (1) establish their goals, (2) shape their instruction to hug and bridge closer to the transfer desired, and (3) "deliberately provoke students to think about how they approach tasks."[7] Adapting PACT to the ACRL concept of Research as Inquiry can hug, bridge, and provoke reflection about what it means to reflection about what it means to contribute to a scholarly conversation.

With Kara and your other students in mind, your goal is clear: you want to help your students transfer their effective writing strategies into effective research strategies. You want to teach in ways that will promote this transfer. Thank goodness you are team-teaching this semester with one of the university librarians!

As the two of you work on some new lessons, you keep in mind that Perkins and Salomon suggest that transfer depends on explicit instruction, on analogies, on patterns and principles that organize knowledge, and on self-reflection.[8] By shaping instruction to hug and bridge PACT and the Research as Inquiry framework closer to the transfer of written literacy to information literacy, the lesson comes together.

Explicit instruction will involve discussing the ACRL Research as Inquiry framework with our students to be sure they understand the goals, practices, and dispositions. It will also involve a brief lecture on the differences and similarities among peer-reviewed, trade, and popular journal articles.

Analogies may include Perkins and Salomon's concepts of hugging and bridging, but you also want to extend the analogy you see in the ACRL framework Research as *Exploration.* What set of documents might we explore together as a class so that we can collectively ask questions and develop new research, analysis, and evaluation strategies? We decided to create a sample set of peer-reviewed, trade, and popular journal articles that all center on the same topic.

We can also extend the metaphoric sense of PACT. As writers, your students have already practiced using simple questions about purpose, audience, conventions, and trouble spots. PACT can also work in the sense of brokering a relationship between writing and research. Writerly questions about purpose, audience, conventions, and trouble spots closely connect to source evaluation (i.e., hugging for transfer). Students can easily ask, "What is the *purpose* of each source?" As a teacher, you can help them bridge a little farther (for transfer to research) by asking them to notice *where* they find that sense of purpose as they read a source. You are equally certain that your students can ask, "Who is the intended *audience* for this source?" Again, you can bridge this question a little farther toward helping students look for audience clues within their sources. What, for instance, can they glean from the publication *conventions* for the source? You already have students keep track of their difficulties in finding or evaluating sources. What if you also asked students to consider *trouble spots* in terms of when the source would be useful or inappropriate?

As students like Kara find answers to familiar PACT questions not only as writers but also as researchers, they will almost certainly find themselves asking new questions of their own. When Kara is able to ask questions based on information gaps or conflicting perspectives (one of the knowledge practices the ACRL frameworks associate with Research as Inquiry), she will have crossed a bridge. She will have traveled beyond her familiar research terrain. Rather than patching together random sources without fully understanding them, Kara will be developing the strategies she needs to transfer her abilities as a writer and reader to scholarly research. Extending the PACT questions to research will help students evaluate sources more fully while reflecting on their own research processes and goals; as a result, strong literacy practices will transfer to strong information literacy practices.

Lesson Plan

Learner Analysis

- This lesson works well with advanced first-year students and upper-division students. Advanced skills necessary for successful completion include the ability to quickly and accurately analyze articles from peer-reviewed, trade, and popular journals, examining not only content but also publication information and design, among other elements. Additional skills include categorizing publication types using this analysis as well as evaluating each article's purpose, audience, publication context, and potential research trouble spots.

Orienting Context and Prerequisites

Learner prerequisites

- Students should come to the session with potential research topics.

Instructional Context

- This session should be held in a room that enables students to

move their seating and to work comfortably in groups. The room should also have a whiteboard or chalkboard so that the instructor can create the PACT chart on it and allow students to fill it out.
- If the librarian is wrapping up the class with a database demonstration, a computer podium and projector is necessary.

Pre-instruction setup

- The teaching librarian needs to prepare a brief lecture on the differences and similarities among peer-reviewed, trade, and popular journal articles.
- The teaching librarian needs to find a peer-reviewed, trade, and popular journal article ideally about the same topic. Having articles from different publication types that focus on the same topic demonstrates to students how different publication genres present the same topic. Ideally, these articles should lend themselves to be scanned and analyzed quickly during a regular class session.
- The teaching librarian needs to make enough copies of each article for students in class or enough copies for each group.
- Before the class starts, the librarian creates the PACT chart on the board.

Learning Outcomes and Activities

Learning Outcomes

1. Students will understand the value in and the use of multiple perspectives available in differing publication types and implement this understanding during information gathering and assessment.
2. Students will explain the differences and similarities among popular, trade, and peer-reviewed journals in regard to each publication type's purpose, audience, publication conventions, and research trouble spots.

Learning Activities

Students will:

- Analyze sample articles for their purpose, audience, publication conventions, and potential trouble spots (PACT) for a researcher

- Categorize articles as either peer-reviewed, trade, or popular based on analysis for PACT.
- Identify appropriate source types based on the scope and audience for their research plan.

1. Group Work/Discussion *(LO2, 50 minutes, essential)*
    - Show students definitions of peer-reviewed, trade, and popular sources on the board/screen and briefly discuss.
    - Put students in four groups.
    - Give each group either a sample peer-reviewed, trade, or popular article on the same topic.
    - Ask students to determine the following, using evidence from the articles to support their assertions:
        a. Was the article published in a peer-reviewed, trade, and popular journal?
        b. What is the *purpose* of the article?
        c. Who is the *audience* for the article?
        d. What are the publication *conventions* of the article? (Is the language formal, informal? Are there citations? Pictures?)
        e. What about *trouble spots*? In what circumstances can each article be useful? When would the source be inappropriate?
    - Each group shares responses with the class and the librarian notes answers on the board or projects them on a screen from a computer.

Sample Articles for Group Work

- Weiss, Emily, Katherine Miller, Heather Mohan-Gibbons, and Carla Vela. "Why Did You Choose This Pet?: Adopters and Pet Selection Preferences in Five Animal Shelters in the United States." *Animals: An Open Access Journal from Mdpi* 2 (2) (2012): 144–59. doi:10.3390/ani2020144.
- Butcher, Sterry. "Cat Power." *Texas Monthly* (July 2014): 66–69. Available from https://www.texasmonthly.com/the-culture/cat-power/.
- Whitford, Ronald E. "A Solution for Decreased Feline Visits." *DVM Newsmagazine* (September 2011): 89.

2. Search Term Brainstorming and Database Demonstration/Workshop *(LO1, 15 minutes, essential)*
   - Students write down their working research plan, thinking about the types of information that they need. Briefly work on revising their list and where they can find that information, based on what they have learned from the activity.
   - Librarian picks two or three students to share revisions with class.

Assessment

Assessment goals

Students will successfully analyze articles as to their purpose, audience, conventions, and potential research trouble spots and use this information to accurately categorize three articles as popular, trade, or scholarly, but also understand the potential and contextual utility of each publication type. Students will see research questions and research resources as modes for further inquiry. As students work with resources, this activity should encourage them to critically engage with and interrogate each source as to its usefulness.

Assessment tool(s)

Formative assessment is utilized in class through the use of the PACT chart and the librarian-led and -facilitated discussion. As students discuss the articles and definitions, the librarian completes the PACT chart to track student understanding. S/he can reinforce correct analysis and categorization as well as rectify incorrect analysis and categorization through further discussion.

PACT Chart

	Publication Type?	**Purpose?**	**Audience?**	**Publication Conventions?**	**Potential Trouble-Spots?**
Article 1					
Article 2					
Article 3					

Summative assessment occurs when students apply what they have learned in the previous activity to create a research plan that includes not only research questions to be answered but also the types of sources in which that information might be found.

Authentic assessment can be provided using an evaluative rubric that measures the students' inclusion of performance criteria in the final research essay. Note that the following rubric assesses not only the students' evaluation of outside information but also whether they researched and addressed multiple perspectives surrounding their essay topics.

Evaluation Rubric (see Appendix 5A)

- A clear sense of audience and purpose
- Clear and focused assertion
- Accurate and clear synthesis of information in the texts as well as thoughtful and insightful evaluation of the differing perspectives. Supporting information is appropriate to the purpose(s) and audience(s)
- Effective use of rhetoric to establish credibility and authority of the writer for the chosen audience
- Strategic exploration of ideas, sources, and processes
- Careful consideration of the most appropriate genre (essay, letter, feature article, blog, etc.) and the conventions of form associated with that genre choice
- Control of stylistic conventions (including grammar and punctuation)
- Roughly ~2000 words, or eight pages plus references

Appendix 5A
PACT-based Rubric

EVALUATIVE RUBRIC FOR UNIT 4	
PURPOSE. Clearly conveys a central focus; accurately, clearly, and credibly synthesizes, evaluates, and employs information to support a thesis.	
Emerging ⟷	⟷ **Mastering**
• Does not identify a clear focus or structure, which results in a disorganized evaluation • Does not provides sufficient or appropriate supporting details to persuade or educate readers • Does not evaluate differing perspectives thoroughly	• Clearly and accurately supports assertion through evaluation of the sources as well as subsidiary, embedded, or implicit aspects • Maintains a balance of primary and secondary details and issues without rambling or losing focus. • Recognizes nuances of rhetoric that convey authority, and credibility
AUDIENCE: Identifies and considers **others' perspectives and positions** that are important to evaluating the issue effectively	
Emerging ⟷	⟷ **Mastering**
• Focuses primarily on a single perspective and fails to establish credibility and authority. • Does not consider readers' knowledge, needs, or assumptions (e.g., fails to establish context for the reader or fails to provide supporting details) --or does so superficially.	• Thoroughly addresses and evaluates multiple perspectives noted previously, and establishes additional credibility and accuracy from outside information. • Identifies and addresses the readers' knowledge, needs, or assumptions in ways that fully engage the readers' interest.
CONVENTIONS: Conveys **conclusions, implications, or and consequences** (i.e., offers a clear and reasoned assertion through the synthesis and evaluation of different perspectives)	
Emerging ⟷	⟷ **Mastering**
• Does not follow the format/genre conventions for this situation, have chosen an inappropriate style or mode of delivery (too formal or informal) • Has difficulty with the conventions of grammar, spelling, punctuation, and word usage for this situation • Does not follow the conventions for citation or documentation in this situation • Fails to convey conclusions, implications, or consequences	• Genre conventions are used effectively. The information is well-organized and formatted. • The style is clear, accurate, and well-suited to the intended purpose and audience. • Conventions of mechanics and grammar are correct • Any sources are accurately and ethically acknowledged. • Identifies and discusses conclusions, implications, and consequences considering context, assumptions, data, and evidence. • Objectively reflects upon his or her own assertions.
TROUBLE SPOTS: Anticipates obstacles that could get in the way of what the writer wants to achieve.	
Emerging ⟷	⟷ **Mastering**

• Fails to anticipate obstacles in terms of audience, purpose, and/or conventions. The content may be inadequately developed, incomplete, or compromised by major errors that disrupt or distort meaning. Content may	• Anticipates obstacles and questions • Proofreads/rehearses to present a polished final project that is free of distractions or disruptions.

Notes

1. Rebecca Moore Howard, "A Plagiarism Pentimento," *Journal of Teaching Writing* 11, no. 3 (1993): 233–46.
2. Kurt Schick, "Citation Obsession? Get Over It," *Chronicle of Higher Education*, http://www.chronicle.com/article/Citation-Obsession-Get-Over/129575/.
3. "PACT Questions," *SpeakWrite: Effective Communication across the Curriculum*, West Virginia University, http://speakwrite.wvu.edu/.
4. Association of College and Research Libraries Board, *Framework for Information Literacy for Higher Education*, Association of Research and College Libraries, http://www.ala.org/acrl/standards/ilframework.
5. Kathleen Blake Yancey, Liane Robertson, and Kara Taczak, *Writing Across Contexts: Transfer, Composition, and Sites of Writing* (Logan: Utah State University Press, 2014).
6. David N. Perkins and Gavriel Salomon, "Teaching for Transfer," *Educational Leadership* 46, no.1: (1988): 28.
7. Ibid., 30.
8. Ibid., 30–31.

Bibliography

Association of College and Research Libraries Board. *Framework for Information Literacy for Higher Education*. Association of Research and College Libraries. http://www.ala.org/acrl/standards/ilframework.

Howard, Rebecca Moore. "A Plagiarism Pentimento." *Journal of Teaching Writing* 11, no. 3 (1993): 233–46.

"PACT Questions." *SpeakWrite: Effective Communication across the Curriculum*. West Virginia University. http://speakwrite.wvu.edu/.

Perkins, David N., and Gavriel Salomon. "Teaching for Transfer." *Educational Leadership* 46, no.1: (1988): 22–32.

Schick, Kurt. "Citation Obsession? Get Over It." *Chronicle of Higher Education*. http://www.chronicle.com/article/Citation-Obsession-Get-Over/129575/.

Yancey, Kathleen Blake, Liane Robertson, and Kara Taczak. *Writing Across Contexts: Transfer, Composition, and Sites of Writing*. Logan: Utah State University Press, 2014.

CHAPTER 6

Behind the Headlines:

Current Events Topic Discovery and Exploration Using Historical Event Headlines

Mary K. Oberlies
Undergraduate Engagement Librarian
University of Oregon

ACRL Information Literacy Frame: Research as Inquiry
Discipline: Social Sciences
Subjects: Conflict Resolution; Sociology; Criminology; Interdisciplinary
Learning Theory: Constructivism
Instructional Strategy: Vygotsky's Zone of Proximal Development
Special Populations: Non-Traditional Students; Graduate Students; Undergraduate Students; Professional Students

Selecting topics can be difficult for undergraduates. In my experience, they come to me with grand ideas—they want to solve the world's problems in a single go—which are awesome but not realistic. Whenever students come to me with a broad research topic but are struggling to figure out what their research question should be, I encourage them to search for the topic in newspapers. This provides them with various viewpoints on the topic and gives them background information, personal accounts, and a timeline of events. Newspaper articles will also, at times, link the event to other similar events from the past or even legislation. Whenever I mention this to students, they give me a strange look because they often do not see how newspaper articles will get them anywhere with their research.

I wanted to develop a lesson to inspire students to look at current events for topic discovery and exploration. At the time I developed this lesson plan, events in Ferguson, Missouri were front page news, so I pulled historical headlines about the 1992 Los Angeles riots because the events were similar in nature and demonstrated how the issues of police brutality and militarization were not recent phenomena. Guided conversation then enabled students to draw correlations between these similar events.

This particular lesson, developed for upper-level undergraduates taking their first research methods course, prepares students for their capstone course research project. The end project for the class is a research plan for the capstone. This assignment helps students learn how to go from the topic stage to developing research questions by gathering background information. The idea for this lesson came from previous work with a faculty member while I was serving as the Conflict and Peace Studies Librarian at George Mason University. The faculty member asked me to work with her section of this research methods course on gathering data, particularly conducting newspaper and gray literature searches for background information on four current event case studies.

Developing the Lesson Plan

This lesson relies on active group work and is structured for a 100-minute session. Students are broken out into groups of three to four and are given a newspaper article (one copy per student). Each group receives a different article that covers the 1992 Los Angeles riots. The librarian selects the newspaper articles the students will be using so it is possible to alter the lesson to match the discipline of the students. Students read and discuss the article in their groups and brainstorm topics for further exploration. Each group writes their ideas on a whiteboard, which provides real-time authentic assessment and facilitates group discussion. Following the brainstorming session, the groups describe their article and how they can develop potential research topics. It is always interesting to see the range of ideas the groups generate. For example, in one session, some considered exploring legislation, community response to riots, police responses and militarization, civil rights, and linkages to the 2014 Ferguson riots.

Following this, I lead a discussion about conducting research on interdisciplinary topics, developing keywords, identifying databases, and evaluating sources. During this discussion student participation is activated by asking leading questions that require students to demonstrate their prior knowledge of conducting and understanding research. For example: What are keywords? How do we use Boolean operators? When do you use a book versus a journal article? How do you determine what type of information is needed for your question? I then ask the groups to create a research plan (Appendix 6A) on one of their identified topics; this can be done individually or in pairs.

After creating a research plan, each group shares their plan with the class. This allows me to do an authentic assessment of whether the students understand the discussion and provide corrections as needed. For the remainder of the session, students try their searches out and find three articles, evaluate them (Appendix 6B), and share one article with the class and why they selected it.

Instructional Strategy: The Zone of Proximal Development

The benefit to this lesson is that it reflects the real-world nature of research, while in college it becomes natural to lean on the assistance of professors to either provide a topic for research or provide guidance on topics. Once out of school, inquiry is prompted when students see problems and think of ways to respond to them. Newspapers can stimulate idea formation in students by helping them identify current real-world problems, understand how different populations respond to these issues, and apply their own experiences for sense-making. This focus on sense-making through learned experiences is a foundation of constructivist theory. "Learners… are not empty vessels waiting to be filled, but rather active organisms seeking meaning."[1] Students will grapple with what they encounter until they make sense of the information and construct new understandings. An added benefit to teaching with newspaper articles is that it is an information medium students will encounter for the rest of their lives (assuming newspapers continue to be published). Knowledge must be continually developed through problem solving and encountering challenges to previous understandings.[2] This matches Vygotsky's theory of learning—that real-world problems naturally encourage learning, so by including them in instruction we can improve learning.[3] With newspapers, students are using a tool they will likely use to exchange ideas with their peers outside the educational environment. This encourages learning along Vygotsky's zone of proximal development (ZPD) and constructivist theory.

Learning Theory: Constructivism

Instruction following the constructivist learning theory allows students to be active participants in the learning process. The teacher is not the expert but instead acts as a guide, facilitating students to test their knowledge. A lesson plan based on constructivism includes active learning, collaboration, and consideration that each student has prior knowledge and meanings that they bring with them into the learning environment.[4] The key element to constructivist instruction is allowing students to establish their own learning goals through problem solving.

> The main activity in a constructivist classroom is solving problems. Students use inquiry methods to ask questions, investigate a topic, and use a variety of resources to find solutions and answers. As students explore the topic, they draw conclusions, and, as exploration continues, they revisit those conclusions. Exploration of questions leads to more questions.[5]

Mentioned earlier, an underlying instructional strategy in this lesson is Vygotsky's ZPD. Just as with constructivism, ZPD encourages problem solving using past experiences to expand learning.[6] Since students bring their prior knowledge into the learning environment, lessons utilizing collaborative work and problem solving create a zone of proximal development. In this, students go from a level they can successfully reach with independent problem solving to a zone they could reach with the guidance and collaboration of more capable peers.[7] Through the assistance of the librarian and peers, students have opportunities to expand their skills into the zone of proximal development. According to Vygotsky's theory of learning, "learning leads development," meaning that learning should motivate us and through this reach new levels of knowledge.[8] This lesson encourages learning through motivation by tapping students' experiences and understanding of current events and asking them to explore and research solutions to the problems they identify.

ACRL Information Literacy Frame: Research as Inquiry

This lesson works within the frame Research as Inquiry. Instruction within this frame encourages students to discover the following:

1. Research requires continual engagement and exploration with information.
2. They must keep looking for gaps in information and re-examining information from various lenses.
3. Research goes beyond academic course requirements; skills translate to personal, professional, and society inquiry.
4. Research is collaborative and crosses disciplinary boundaries.
5. Disagreements and debate within research deepens conversation and expands knowledge.[9]

By using historical events, the lesson demonstrates the evolution of issues. Police brutality is obviously not a new phenomenon, but by starting with the 1992 Los Angeles riots, students might see how police militarization developed. Reading the headlines of this event helps them further engage with similar current events. Students learn to ask themselves: How are these events similar? What were the different responses to the riots? How did the public and political reactions to the 1992 Los Angeles riots influence public, political, and law enforcement responses to the 2014 Ferguson riots? Students, especially typically aged undergraduates, might lack the knowledge of the 1992 Los Angeles riots, so this lesson can help them to look at other historical events. This teaches them to look for gaps in information: What other incidents like this have happened? What have scholars and public officials said about these events? What public policy has been created in response to them?

The collaborative nature of this instruction session demonstrates the real atmosphere of research. Working as a group, the students examine an event and identify topics for investigation. These topics are generally center around attempting to fix problems or effectively respond to them. In sharing what each group comes up with, students learn that there are multiple ways to examine a situation, deepening their knowledge. By creating a research plan where they must identify the disciplines their topic touches on, they see how research crosses disciplinary boundaries, expanding their field of investigation and the scholarly debates they encounter.

Lesson Plan: Using the News to Find Your Topic

Best- and Worst-Case Scenarios

In a perfect scenario, students are engaged and will also see how past events inform decisions and reactions that influence future events. This goes beyond preparing them for conducting research and encourages them to be informed citizens.

In a worst-case scenario, student attitudes derail the class; however, I have only experienced this once with this lesson. Students got frustrated that they were not getting to devote the entire session to finding articles for their individual research and failed to see how the skills in this lesson would transfer. In this case, the session was held later in the semester, and my session was being used as a substitute for their normal class while the professor was at a conference. This can be rectified by more communication between the librarian and instructor and scheduling the session on a day with the instructor present to reinforce the value of it.

Learner Analysis

- This lesson plan is best suited for upper-level undergraduates, first-year graduate students, professional students, and non-traditional students. It requires a level of prior knowledge in current events, basic skills in research, and ability to synthesis information. Upper-level undergraduates should have learned many of these skills, having completed research papers and becoming knowledgeable in their field of study. First-year graduate students often just need to brush up on their research skills, and this lesson is a great way to reintroduce them to topic development and prepare them to engage further in their field of research. Professional and non-traditional students come with additional skills and knowledge learned from their working environment and, potentially, field experience. For these students, using past and current events as a platform to jumpstart research can be comforting because it removes the fear of the unknown and encourages them to use and share their knowledge with the group. Group activities allow each student to bring their own experiences and abilities to the table, thereby creating a more inclusive environment.

- Students need to be able to handle self-directed tasks. It would be a good idea to check with the faculty instructor to see if this type of lesson is appropriate for his/her class. The librarian should expect to be monitoring group activity.

Orienting Context and Prerequisites

- There are no pre-instruction learning tasks.
- Prerequisites for this class include knowledge of current events, experience exploring and developing topics, and ability to synthesize information.

Instructional Context

- The optimal space for this lesson is a room designed for group work, with moveable tables and chairs, and several white boards or wall space for flipchart paper. Students must have computer access. The librarian should have access to a computer and projector when leading discussion and highlighting library resources (LibGuides, etc.) between the group breakout sessions.
- Prior to instruction, the librarian will need to identify a significant past event that played out in the news headlines. This event must correlate to current events. Depending on the size of the class, the librarian will need to find four or five news articles about this event, one article per group, and make sure each student in each group gets a copy of the article. It is important that the librarian has read through each article to take into consideration whether there is potential that any students will be sensitive to the events covered. I recommend the librarian prepare a list of topic ideas for each article in case they are needed by the students, and to explain the correlation between the past event and current events.

Learning Outcomes and Activities

Learning Outcomes

1. After attending this library instruction session, the student will be able to identify a topic for further exploration.
2. After attending this library instruction session, the student will be able to construct an appropriate search strategy and locate three resources relevant to their topic.
3. After attending this library instruction session, the student will be able to evaluate three resources and explain how they meet the needs of his/her research.

Learning Activities

1. Students work within groups to read and discuss the newspaper articles provided and brainstorm potential topics for further inquiry. Students should display their ideas using notepads or whiteboards *(LO1,10–20 minutes, essential).*
2. The librarian facilitates a group discussion with the class about the news articles and the topics identified, including how they came up with the ideas and thought processes *(LO1, 5 minutes, essential).*
3. The librarian leads a discussion about conducting research, including how to identify keywords, Boolean operators, how to select effective sources for research, and evaluation information *(LO1-3, 10–15 minutes, essential).*
4. Using information just discussed, students work in their groups to create a research plan for one brainstormed topic (Appendix 6A) *(LO1-2, 5–10 minutes, essential).*
   - Students conduct searches based on the research plan they created and locate three articles relevant to the topic *(LO2, 10–20 minutes, non-essential).*
     - ▷ This activity could become an after-session assignment, which is sent to the librarian for review and feedback if time is no available during the session.
5. After students have completed their searches, each group shares one article they found with the class, explaining how they found it and determined it was an appropriate source for their topic (Appendix 6B) *(LO3, 5–10 minutes, non-essential).*

- If time is not available during the session, this activity could become an after-session assignment, which is sent to the librarian for review and feedback.

Assessment

During this instruction session, I assessed the students'

- ability to identify topics for further exploration;
- understanding of research and how to create a research plan;
- ability to create a successful search strategy; and
- ability to evaluate information and articulate this to peers.

Assessment Tools

- Assessment is primarily derived from student discussion following group work and during the librarian-led session. Students are asked to discuss their article, how they came up with their topics, how they plan to research the topic, and at the conclusion of the instruction session what they found after searching and how it was relevant to their needs.
- Optional Formal Assessment Tool: Have students submit their topic, research plan, and three articles they found with an explanation of why they selected those articles to the librarian following the session. This is evaluated by the librarian to assess whether the students achieved the learning outcomes.
- The session is considered successful if the students are able to do the following:
    1. Articulate how they identified their topics for further exploration from the news article and that the topics are relevant to what they read. Relating this back to current events/policies is considered very successful.
    2. Create a successful research plan that contains relevant keywords, with at least one synonym for each keyword, the disciplines their topic crosses, and at least three databases they would search in.
    3. Locate three articles and explain how these articles are relevant to their topic and will assist them in further their research.

Appendix 6A
Creating a Research Plan

A research plan can help you organize your thoughts and guide your research process from start to finish. By thinking about what questions you need to answer, the type of sources needed, and identifying databases to start your search before beginning the process, it can help you stay on track and avoid becoming overwhelmed with all the information out there.

As a group, select one of the topic ideas you generated based on the articles you read and complete the following questions.

What questions do you have about this topic? What do you want to know more about?	
What type of information do you need to find to answer the questions you just identified? *For example: Will you need government documents? Historical information? Statistics? Journal articles or policy briefs?*	
What disciplines (subject areas) does your topic cover? *For example: Criminology? Sociology? Political Science? Law?*	
What are some basic keywords you might use to search for information on this topic? What are 1–2 synonyms for each keyword?	
What databases might you use? *The University Libraries have great subject guides* (http://infoguides.gmu.edu) *which provide recommendations on databases. Take a look at some of the guides within the disciplines you identified previously.*	

Appendix 6B
Evaluating Sources

Conduct a search using the keywords and one of the databases you identified in your research plan. Locate three articles that could be used to answer your question or help you dig deeper into your topic. Use the CRAAPP Test to evaluate your articles:

> **C**urrency: When was this published? Has it been revised? Can you use older sources or should they be within the last ten years?
>
> **R**elevance: Does the information relate to your topic or answer your question? Who is the intended audience? Is this information appropriate for you to be citing in a research paper?
>
> **A**uthority: Who is the author/source of the information? Is the author qualified to be writing on this topic?
>
> **A**ccuracy: Where does this information come from? Is it supported by evidence? Has it been reviewed (peer-reviewed)? What type of language is being used? Is it free of errors, free of emotion, and is there bias?
>
> **P**urpose: What is the intent of the information? Is the point of view objective? Is the information meant to teach, inform, persuade, or entertain?
>
> **P**ublication: Who published this information? Is it scholarly? Is it a magazine, blog, or social media? Is it the result of scholarly research but not reviewed (dissertation, government document, gray literature)?

Enter the citation for the 3 articles you found:	Evaluate the source. What makes it a good source for your question? Use the CRAAPP method above.
1.	
2.	

Notes

1. Marcy P. Driscoll, *Psychology of Learning for Instruction* (Needham Heights: Allyn & Bacon, 2000): 376.
2. Ibid., 379.
3. Ibid., 250.
4. Barbara Blummer, "Applying Perkins's Facets of a Learning Environment for Information Literacy Instruction," *Community & Junior College Libraries* 14, no. 3 (January 2008): 181, doi: 10.1080/02763910802035108.
5. UCD Teaching and Learning, "Education Theory: Constructivism and Social Constructivism in the Classroom," *Open Educational Resources of UCD Teaching and Learning, University College Dublin,* accessed December 8, 2015, http://www.ucdoer.ie/index.php/Education_Theory/Constructivism_and_Social_Constructivism_in_the_Classroom.
6. Driscoll, 250.
7. Tony Harland, "Vygotsky's Zone of Proximal Development and Problem-Based Learning: Linking a Theoretical Concept with Practice Through Action Research," *Teaching in Higher Education*, 8, no. 2 (2003): 264–65, doi: 10.1080/1356251032000052483.
8. Fred Newman and Lois Holzman, *Lev Vygotsky: Revolutionary Scientist* (New York: Routledge, 1993): 60.
9. Association of College & Research Libraries (ACRL), *Framework for Information Literacy for Higher Education*, 2015, accessed March 3, 2017, http://www.ala.org/acrl/standards/ilframework#inquiry.

Bibliography

Association of College & Research Libraries (ACRL). *Framework for Information Literacy for Higher Education.* Text, 2015. Accessed March 3, 2017. http://www.ala.org/acrl/standards/ilframework#inquiry.

Blummer, Barbara. "Applying Perkins's Facets of a Learning Environment for Information Literacy Instruction." *Community & Junior College Libraries* 14, no. 3 (2008): 179–89. doi:10.1080/02763910802035108.

Driscoll, Marcy P. *Psychology of Learning for Instruction.* Needham Heights: Allyn & Bacon, 2000.

Harland, Tony. “Vygotsky’s Zone of Proximal Development and Problem-Based Learning: Linking a Theoretical Concept with Practice Through Action Research.” *Teaching in Higher Education* 8, no. 2 (2003): 263–72. doi:10.1080/1356251032000052483.

Newman, Fred, and Lois Holzman, *Lev Vygotsky: Revolutionary Scientist*. New York: Routledge, 1993.

UCD Teaching and Learning. “Education Theory/Constructivism and Social Constructivism in the Classroom.” *Open Educational Resources of UCD Teaching and Learning, University College Dublin*. Accessed December 8, 2015. http://www.ucdoer.ie/index.php/Education_Theory/Constructivism_and_Social_Constructivism_in_the_Classroom.

CHAPTER 7

Research as Inquiry:
A Strategy for Questioning

Sharon Radcliff
Associate Librarian
California State University, East Bay

ACRL Information Literacy Frame: Research as Inquiry
Discipline: Social Sciences; Humanities
Subject: Global Issues; English; History; Social Studies
Learning Theories: Reading Response Theory; Social Constructivism
Pedagogy: Inquiry-Based Learning
Special Populations: Undergraduate Students; Multicultural/Diversity

ACRL Information Literacy Frame: Research as Inquiry

According to ACRL's *Framework for Information Literacy for Higher Education*,[1] "Research is iterative and depends on asking increasingly complex or new questions whose answers, in turn, develop additional questions or lines of inquiry in any field." A question for the information literacy practitioner is: How can students learn to develop "increasingly complex question or lines of inquiry"? The most dominant method of developing questions of increasing cognitive complexity is, of course, the ubiquitous "Bloom's Taxonomy," recently revised[2] to consist of the following kinds of skills (around which questions and exercises may be built):

- Remember
- Understand
- Apply
- Analyze
- Evaluate
- Create

Learning Theory and Pedagogy: Reading Response and Inquiry-Based Learning

However, another possibility, which places the locus of question development on the student instead of the instructor in a rather novel way, which is described in this chapter, is to teach students how to create questions based on the Christenbury and Kelly "Questioning Circle" method. This method acknowledges the reader response theory of reading, popularized by Louise Rosenblatt,[3] which regards reading as a transaction between the text and reader, where meaning is created from the interaction of the reader's background and the text.

The questioning circle method trains students to develop questions based on a text, their knowledge of the world and of the subject matter, and their own experiences. These three distinct areas can form the basis of simple questions but may also be combined to create more complex questions of the following types:

- text/reader experience
- text/knowledge of the world
- knowledge of the world/ reader experience

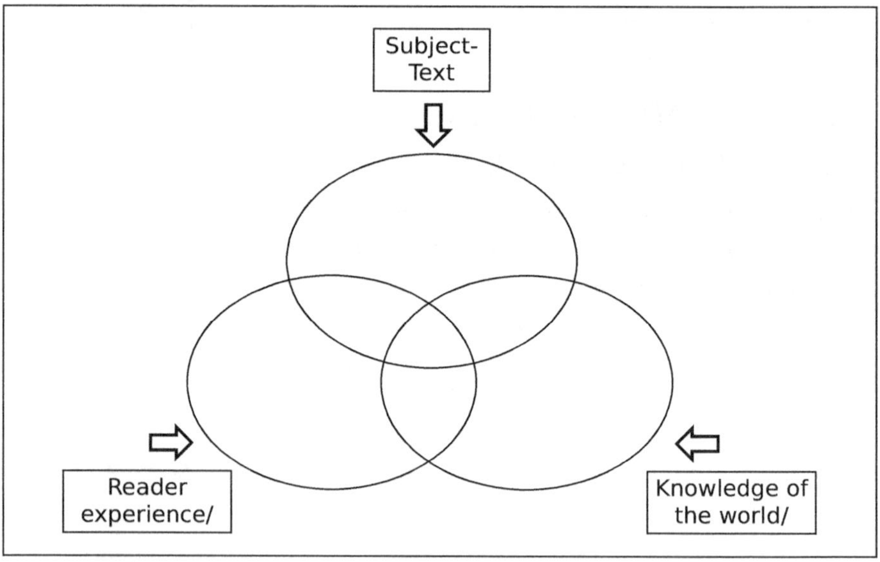

Figure 7.1: Venn Diagram illustrating Questioning Circle Method.
(Christenbury & Kelly)

All three kinds of questions may be combined into what the technique describes as a "dense" question. In the above diagram, this is shown by the intersection of all three circles. These questions push the level of inquiry forward in the manner described in the framework and so that even "novice learners acquire strategic perspectives on inquiry and a greater repertoire of investigative methods."[4]

Generally, this method is flexible enough to be used in a variety of subject area courses at a variety of levels with students from diverse backgrounds. In fact, it is especially useful for harnessing a diversity of backgrounds in the classroom, as the method engages students in understanding material both through the lens of their own experiences and through their collective research into concepts from the reading that may lie beyond their collective understanding.

My own experience with the method has been in community college developmental level English courses and in state university's first-year, two-unit information literacy course. In both cases, the students were very diverse, and in the case of the community college environment, many were learning English as a second or third language. Because I was the teacher of record for the course, I had the luxury of integrating instruction in the questioning circle method into several class sessions using a variety of reading materials, including poetry, short narrative essays, and a novel. The state university information literacy class is part of a first-year cluster of general education courses aligned around a theme, such as "making a difference" (social sciences), "bodies in motion" (kinesiology), or "energy and the environment" (sciences). Depending on the theme, a variety of readings may be used in the context of the questioning circle method. Coordination with faculty teaching other sections included in the cluster is also possible, though I have not tried this out.

If this method is used as a one- or two-hour session integrated into a course taught by another faculty member, the faculty member would have to assign the reading material beforehand and allow for time to instruct students both in the questioning circle method and in the research skills necessary to answer knowledge-based questions about the material that go beyond the students' own knowledge. But the beauty of this method is it may be used with any readings assigned already in a course, so no additional reading assignment is needed. If this method is used in a one-shot session, it would be desirable to "flip" the lecture and have students view information about the questioning circle method online before class.

A strong benefit of the method is that students are able to initiate and guide the direction of inquiry based both on interest and their need to expand their own knowledge in order to understand the material. The method may be used with both fiction and non-fiction material. In my courses, I introduced the method after the course had been in session for three to four weeks, and students had already been exposed to the reading material and have already answered some questions about the readings. It is also desirable, but not always possible, to have students answer some questions generated by the method before attempting to create their own.

Learning Theory: Social Constructivism

This technique may be taught in an especially effective way in the context of group work, incorporating a social constructivist approach developed by theorists such as Vygotsky and related to Piaget's cognitive constructivism. According to Palincsar,[5] "Social constructivist perspectives focus on the interdependence of social and individual processes in the co-construction of knowledge." He goes on to state that both Piaget and Vygotsky's views suggest that the interpersonal and cross-cultural communication of students is as important to the learning outcome as is the instruction itself, hence the efficacy of using groups as the setting for generating and discussing questions developed using the questioning circle method, which in and of itself provides a structure for integrating background knowledge and personal experience into the equation of understanding, investigating and finding new lines of inquiry within, and from textual material.

This methodology, although providing the scaffolding for rich and complex student-generated questions leading to equally diverse and complex discussion and investigations, can be taught in a fairly simple way to begin with. For example, here is how students may be taught to generate questions using a poem. Students may be given a short poem, chosen to be relevant to your student population group. I have often used poems by Tupac Shakur (e.g., "A Rose Grows in Concrete" or "Liberty Needs Glasses"), Gwendolyn Brooks (e.g., "We Jazz June"), William Carlos Williams (e.g., "The Wheelbarrow"), and Langston Hughes (e.g., "Dream Deferred"), among others, for this purpose.

Consider Tupac Shakur's poem: "Lady Liberty Needs Glasses."[6] Students may find these lines of interest:

excuse me but lady liberty needs glasses
and so does mrs justice by her side
both the broads r blind as bats
stumbling thru the system

Typically, students will be able to generate both "shaded" and "dense" questions such as:

Shaded

1. What do "lady liberty" and "mrs justice" both symbolize? (text and knowledge of the world)
2. Have I ever felt like how the narrator seems to feel, disappointed about the political system? (text, reader experience)
3. Could I write a poem about something I had strong emotions or ideas about? (Reader experience/knowledge of the world)

Dense

1. What kind of reactions would different people have to this poem? (text, knowledge of the world, reader experience)

The next few lines…

justice bumbed into mutulu and
trippin on geronimo pratt
but stepped right over oliver
and his crooked partner ronnie

justice stubbed her big toe on mandela

create many opportunities for inquiry and exploration in the area of text/knowledge of the world questions, as students may become curious about who the people mentioned are.

This is where the lesson would turn to library database and web searching with further questions relating to reliability, verifiability of sources. Questions about the reliability of sources may also be student generated.

To teach the method, very short and accessible poems work best at the beginning; more complex poems may be introduced later. Short fiction and non-fiction works may also be used when chosen for both relevance to the course subject matter and to students' background, experiences, and interests. Short biographical works by authors from a diverse background who write specifically about their experiences in education and learning—for example, Amy Tan, Malcolm X, Sherman Alexie, Toni Morrison, etc.—are good choices for generating questions using this methodology as students may readily apply and see parallels with a biographical narrative to their own knowledge and experiences while finding paths of inquiry to pursue.

In courses where students are reading novels or longer fictional works, these works may also be used to generated questions. For example, the novel *Secret Life of Bees* by Sue Monk Kidd works well and allows students to generate their own questions on a variety of themes, including racism, the history of the civil rights movement, sisterhood, morality, and religion.

Here are examples of the kinds of questions student have generated for this work, using the Questioning Circle method:

Simple

- Text: Why won't June marry Neil? How did Lily's and June's relationship change? (Questions about character's motivation and character relationships.)
- Reader experience: Have you ever had a police officer bully you? (Rosaleen is bullied by the police during the civil rights movement in the South.)
- World knowledge: When did ice cream cost a nickel? Is it hard to harvest honey?

Shaded

- Text/experience: How do you feel about Rosaleen being a victim of racism? If you did not have any money like Lily would you steal?
- Text/knowledge of the world: Do you think the world is still prejudiced? Why was there racism in the 1960s and how does it differ from today's racism?
- Reader's experience/knowledge of the world: How important is family? How has religion changed the world?

Dense questions

Reader's experience/knowledge of the world/text:

- Do you think T-Ray is telling Lily the truth about her mother or is he trying to hurt her?
- (To answer this, you need to use the book, your knowledge of father-daughter relationships, and your reaction to the book's dialogue.)
- If you were left at the altar like June on your wedding day, would you also decide to never marry?
- How do you think people will change as a result of reading this book?
- What would you do if you were left with no money like Lily and Rosaleen?
- If you were Rosaleen, would you stand up for Lily?

This method creates a very rich learning experience for students as they work in groups to both create and answer questions that draw upon their shared knowledge and individual experiences. It is important in choosing material to consider multi-cultural texts and essays written on current topics, supplementing textbook readings with current articles. This can be done in collaboration with subject-area faculty so that appropriate articles and/or poems are chosen for the questioning circle method workshop(s). Overall, this approach creates an environment of mutual respect in the classroom in which students are encouraged to express their own perspectives on classroom material. Some advantages of using this methodology to explore texts and subject matter are:

- Students are more invested in creating and answering classmates' questions than in writing out responses to yours.
- Students develop critical thinking and meta-cognitive skills via the process of generating questions using this model.
- Students can learn the model quickly because it is conceptually simple but when applied to a subject matter or text quickly becomes very complex.

In fact, I am often surprised by the direction students take with their questioning, realizing that they have found significance in part of the text that I have overlooked. Some difficulties of using this method include:

- Students may initially be uncomfortable generating their own questions and sharing them with peers.
- Students may learn the process at different rates; some students will have trouble with shaded and dense questions.

- The process can become repetitive so should be varied with teacher questions, writing questions on the board, etc.
- Poetry may be chosen to illustrate social or historical themes, which could affect the daily lives of students, thus creating interest, the ability to generate relevant questions, and create paths of inquiry leading to using library databases for research, depending on the subject area and context of the lesson.

Lesson Plan

Learner Analysis

- This approach works well with first-year college students, including students who are in developmental-level courses for English.
- The focus on reader experience and knowledge of the world also welcomes a diversity of backgrounds and viewpoints and thus is ideal for use with a diverse student population.
- This questioning methodology puts the locus of learning on the student. Having students generate questions that incorporate and value their own experience while developing and building on their knowledge of the world (in relation to the text) is highly motivating for learning as students may hone in on areas of interest while learning both about others' viewpoints and the subject at hand.
- The main limitation is that by giving over the process of inquiry to the students, even in a structured way, the instructor does lose the ability to choose the focus of inquiry and discourse; however, the value of re-centering learning on the students probably outweighs this limitation.

Orienting Context and Prerequisites

- Ideally, students need to have been assigned the reading before the class session in which the questioning method is taught.

Instructional Context

- Students need access to the internet, at least one database per group.

- Students need to be trained in the questioning circle method; short pieces of prose or poetry may be used to this end.

Learning Outcomes and Learning Activities

Learning Outcomes

Students will be able to:

1. construct questions about reading material based on the Christenbury Questioning Circle Method;[7]
2. construct and discuss questions based on the text, personal experience, or knowledge of the world;
3. reflect through discussion and writing how personal experiences and background knowledge may influence a reader's understanding of a text; and
4. develop skill in researching knowledge of the world questions, which come out of reading a text.

Learning Activities

1. Interactive Lecture *(LO1, 20 minutes, essential)*
   - An interactive lecture and with visuals via a PowerPoint or handouts introducing the Questioning Circle Method, the three kinds of questions (simple, complex, and dense, combining, text, personal experience, and knowledge of the world) is essential. This could be done as a flipped learning session to be completed online before class if needed to shorten class time. If done this way, the interactive part could be replaced with short "knowledge check" questions. Examples of generating questions would be provided and of answering knowledge-based questions using library databases and evaluating sources using further critical questions (see Appendix 7A).
2. Group Work with Poems *(LO1-3, 30 minutes, essential)*
   - Group work using either poems or articles short enough to be read as part of the group work or using longer material prepared in advice (homework) is also essential. The purpose of the group work is for students to develop a series of questions from simple to complex, using all the areas (text, personal experience, knowledge of the world); then these questions are exchanged between groups. The second half

of the group work is for students to answer the questions posed by the other groups. This is the heart of the lesson and essential. The only variation would be how many questions students are asked to generate and to answer. Also, the format could be face-to-face or online. The deliverables from the group could involve reporting out or creating posters, so even further discussion is generated (see Appendix 7A).

3. Knowledge of the World Questions *(LO4, 20 minutes, essential)*
   - For "knowledge of the world"-based questions, students would be encouraged to use library databases and the WWW to answer these questions, and students would be encouraged to generate critical questions about the quality of sources they find to answer these questions and continue to pursue these lines of inquiry (see Appendix 7A).

Assessment

- Assessment is formative, as in the instructor should check in with the groups periodically.
- More product-orientated assessment could be done by examining the questions and answers created by the students to see if they are fully formed using the Questioning Circle Method.
- The ability of students to answer "knowledge of the world" questions can be assessed by evaluating the kinds of sources used by students to answer these questions.
- Since the method is meant to engage students and encourage students to make meaning by engaging with one another, a survey approach that measures student engagement would also be a useful tool.

Appendix 7A

Simple:
Text based:

Reader Experience:

Knowledge of the World:

Shaded:
Text based: Reader Experience:
Text based/Knowledge of the World:

Reader Experience/Knowledge of the World:

Dense:
Text/Reader Experience/Knowledge of the World

Group Dense Question:

1. Having exchanged your Handout One with your questions with another group, discuss whether each question fits with the given designation. If not try to adjust the question so that it does fit.
2. Discuss and answer the question as a group. If group members have different views on the question include those variations in your response.
3. For the questions involving “knowledge of the world”; first discuss within the group, then come up with a strategy using both library databases and the WWW to verify and or find out more information to complete the answer.
4. For any additional information added to your answers to “knowledge of the world” questions, cite the source and state why you believe this source is reliable.
5. Having both created and answered questions about the poem using this method, what question or questions is your group most interested in pursuing further and what strategy would you use to do this?

Notes

1. ACRL, *Framework for Information Literacy for Higher Education*, http://www.ala.org/acrl/standards/ilframework.
2. David Krathwohl, "A Revision of Bloom's Taxonomy: An Overview," *Theory into Practice*, 41, no 4 (2002): 212–18.
3. Louise Rosenblatt, *Literature as Exploration* (New York: D. Appleton-Century, 1938; New York: MLA, 1995).
4. ACRL, 2010.
5. A. Sullivan Palincsar, "Social Constructivist Perspectives on Teaching and Learning," *Annual Review of Psychology*, 49 (1998): 345–75.
6. Tupac Shakur, *A Rose that Grew from Concrete* (London: Simon & Schuster, UK Ltd, 1998).
7. Leila Christenbury and Patricia Kelly, *Questioning: A Path to Critical Thinking* (Urbana: ERIC Clearinghouse on Reading and Communication Skills and the National Council of Teachers of English,1983).

Bibliography

ACRL. *Framework for Information Literacy for Higher Education.* (2015). http://ala.org/acrl/standards/ilframework.

Christenbury, Leila, and Patricia Kelly. *Questioning: A Path to Critical Thinking.* Urbana: ERIC Clearinghouse on Reading and Communication Skills and the National Council of Teachers of English, 1983: ED 226 372.

Krathwohl, David R. "A Revision of Bloom's Taxonomy: An Overview." *Theory into Practice,* 41(4) (2002): 212–18.

Palincsar, A. Sullivan. "Social Constructivist Perspectives on Teaching and Learning." *Annual Review of Psychology.* 49 (1998): 345–75.

Rosenblatt, Louise. *Literature as Exploration.* New York: MLA 1995. First published 1938 by Appleton-Century (New York).

Shakur, Tupac. *A Rose that Grew from Concrete.* London: Simon & Schuster, UK Ltd., 1998.

CHAPTER 8

"This is Terrifying!": Problem-Based Learning, Information Literacy, and the Zika Virus

Maoria J. Kirker
Instruction & Assessment Coordinator, MSLIS
George Mason University

Janna Mattson
Instructional & Social Science Librarian, MLS
George Mason University

ACRL Information Literacy Frame: Research as Inquiry
Discipline: Sciences & Engineering
Subject: Public Health
Pedagogy: Problem-Based Learning
Special Populations: Advanced Learners; Graduate Students

Over the past few years, George Mason University Libraries have worked with the Honors College—an accelerated undergraduate program that gives students research and service opportunities—to create a collaborative partnership in their freshman research methods class. All Honors College students are required to take this class, and over the course of this partnership, information literacy instruction has become increasingly robust. The libraries' success in this course led to the Honors College reaching out for instruction with students in their University Scholars Institute.

The University Scholars Institute consists of the highest achieving students within the Honors College and enrolls approximately twenty students with each incoming freshman class. When the director of the program contacted the liaison librarian about teaching in their program, he gave free reign on what the approach could be. The theme for the year was "Globalization and Public Health: The Flows of Peoples, Capital, and Crises Across Borders," with a particular focus on the Ebola and Zika viruses. Because students represent a variety of disciplines in the Honors College, the approach for the University Scholars Institute is multidisciplinary, examining how to ask questions and collaborate across disciplines.

The students in this group ranged from sophomores to seniors. Rather than requiring the usual writing assignment, this program culminates in a project that engages students in asking substantial multidisciplinary questions. Because they received information literacy instruction during the freshman research methods course, we selected problem-based learning (PBL) as the teaching strategy because this pedagogy allows students to apply their previous knowledge to challenging scenarios. Not only does PBL afford students the opportunity to approach a topic from multiple disciplines, it also allows students to apply their research skills toward meaningful discoveries. Due to the true-to-life implications of problem solving in PBL, this pedagogy provides for an engaging learning environment absent of a related assignment. We witnessed this engagement when a student commented on the implications of a Zika outbreak in the DC Metro area, "This is terrifying!"

Pedagogy: Problem Based Learning

Problem-based learning (PBL) emerged as a teaching method in medical education. Instructors present patient symptoms and students use an iterative problem-solving process which includes critical reasoning, information seeking, applying new knowledge to the problem, and evaluating the decision-making process.[1] Because its applications exceed the medical classroom, instructors in other fields embrace PBL. Three elements form the foundation of PBL as students: gain knowledge by analyzing the problem, build lifelong learning skills through the learning process, and tackle the problems in small peer groups.[2]

In the information literacy classroom, PBL offers distinct and overlapping advantages to both instructors and students. Using PBL as an instructional method does not necessitate that a research assignment be directly tied to an information literacy session, which frees librarians to think outside the box on instructional topics. The three elements of PBL allow for modifiable instruction—there is no exact way to teach using PBL. It can be adapted to any learning group and learning context. Problem-based learning activates students' prior knowledge, creating a constructivist classroom experience wherein the instructor acts as a facilitator to learning. Students simultaneously engage in self-directed learning and peer learning to determine a solution to a real-world problem. This provides students an opportunity to practice their information literacy skills in a safe space and relevant context; thus, instructors can choose current topics and demonstrate the lifelong value of information literacy skills.

ACRL Information Literacy Frame: Research as Inquiry

This two-part lesson plan emphasizes the frame Research as Inquiry. Students are challenged to collaboratively design a solution to an ill-structured community health problem—responding to a local Zika outbreak—in order to extend knowledge across fields.[3] The iterative research process is highlighted in the two-session format and the use of PBL, a pedagogy that gives space for the learner to engage in "problems or questions in a discipline or between disciplines that are open or unresolved."[4] Second, since the problem scenario's focus is on the public health crisis of a communicable disease outbreak, the stage is set for learners to engage in work that addresses "personal, professional, or societal needs."[5] The problem scenario has real-world applications in that students respond as professionals who work within their communities and with their professional and personal health-related self-interests in mind.

The two-part structure of this lesson also creates a space where learners may develop the knowledge practice of "breaking complex questions into simple ones, limiting the scope of investigations" since the students work first on a single part of the larger, more complex problem of responding to a local Zika outbreak. This scaffolding is provided for the second part of the lesson, which challenges the students to solve the larger problem in order to create a pathway for students to "seek multiple perspectives during information gathering and assessment."[6] Further, when students come together at the end of the second session as a class to discuss their multidisciplinary teams' solutions, the opportunity arises to display the disposition of open minds and critical stances, asking questions of their classmates' decisions and deciding what they would add to their own solutions given this new information. To facilitate this, we put forward a final discussion point: we ask the students what they would change or add to their solutions.

Lesson Plan

Learner Analysis

- This lesson plan is designed for highly motivated learners with advanced critical thinking skills who are willing to engage in research not necessarily directly connected to their own academic disciplines. In addition, the group of students for which this lesson was initially designed has established relationships with each other through their shared classes and activities within George Mason University's Honors College. Group work is less of a challenge for these students who are familiar with each other.

Orienting Context and Prerequisites

- Students should have prior instruction or knowledge in how to conduct research and using library databases.
- Students should read a journal article that outlines a multidisciplinary approach to a public health problem. For this lesson, the students read the article:

  Jacobsen, Kathryn H., A. Alonso Aguirre, Charles L. Bailey, Ancha V. Baranova, Andrew T. Crooks, Arie Croitoru, Paul L. Delamater, et al. "Lessons from the Ebola Outbreak: Action Items for Emerging Infectious Disease Preparedness and Response." EcoHealth 13, no. 1 (March 1, 2016): 200–12. doi:10.1007/s10393-016-1100-5.

- Independent group discussion about the article is optional between the first and second lessons but leads to more engaged learning, more active participation, and deeper understanding of the problem during the second session.

Instructional Context

- This is a face-to-face lesson, and the ideal classroom set-up is for small group work with whiteboards. If whiteboards are not available, large Post-it Notes may be used. Since there is no lecture or demonstration, an instructor computer and projector are not necessary but would be useful to have if students need search strategies demonstrated. Students should bring their own devices.
- Since students are researching and collaborating on their problems as well as presenting their solutions during the class, the bulk of the librarian's work happens before the lesson. This requires the majority of the instructor's time to concentrate on lesson preparation. For the first session, problem scenarios are created for each key player in it. For example, in the Jacobsen article, we identified four key players in the response to the Ebola epidemic that we used as models in a hypothetical, local Zika virus outbreak to create single-focus problem scenarios. These are:
    - ▷ Prevention Group: *You work for USAID's Emerging Pandemic Threats unit and have been asked to create a list of best practices for early detection of the Zika virus. These best practices will be shared and disseminated amongst the D.C. community. Develop a list of best practices, citing at least two sources to justify your choices.*
    - ▷ Socioeconomic Risk Factors Group: *You work for the CDC's Washington Office and are tasked with creating a list of risk factors for a Zika outbreak in the D.C. area. Create an area-specific list of risk factors considering environmental, social, governmental, and economic factors. Include citations for at least two sources to justify your list.*
    - ▷ Public Health Education: *As the Director of the Department of Health for the city of D.C., you are responsible for overseeing communication with the city's population during health-related crises. Create a communications plan for public awareness in the event of a Zika outbreak. Cite at least two sources to justify your choices.*
    - ▷ Treatment: *You are a hospital administrator and your hospital has been designated as an official treatment center in the event of a Zika outbreak in the D.C. area. You need to*

get your staff and facility prepared for patient care. Create a staff education plan on the Zika virus. Cite at least two sources to justify your plan.

- For session two, we use a prompt that allows the individual groups to join together in multidisciplinary teams. With at least one student from each of the initial groups, the new teams combine their research to propose a solution to a more complex, multidisciplinary problem:
    - ▷ Based on the research you conducted on Monday, create an emergency preparedness plan for a Zika outbreak in the DC area. If you find gaps in your research, choose the appropriate agencies to address the gaps and assign duties/responsibilities to them. These new areas of research can be delegated to those who were not here on Monday. Cite any additional sources used.

Learning Outcomes and Activities

Note: Session one may be used as a standalone lesson; however, the learning outcomes are best supported by both sessions. Session two is not a standalone lesson.

Learning Outcomes

1. Students will seek out evidence to inform challenging decisions while developing an open-minded approach to inquiry.
2. Students will integrate multiple sources and disciplinary perspectives related to a problem to arrive at a multidisciplinary solution.
3. Students incorporate the diverse perspectives that multidisciplinary research provides.

Learning Activities

1. Session One: Learning Activities *(LO1, 75 minutes, essential)*
    - Students self-select their topic—prevention, socioeconomic risk factors, public health education, or treatment. *(5 minutes)*
    - Students identify the resources which will have information related to factors affecting the prevention, spread, and eradication of the Zika virus, e.g., the Center for Disease Control, ScienceDirect, the National Institutes of Health, etc.

The librarian records student responses on the whiteboard. *(5 minutes)*
- Students discuss and research the single-focus problem scenario associated with their chosen topic using at least two sources to support their ideas. *(45 minutes)*
- Each group presents their problem, their proposed solution, and how their sources inform their decision making. The other groups are encouraged to ask questions after each presentation. *(20 minutes)*
- Students hand in their work to the library instructor. *(As students leave)*

2. Session Two: Learning Activities *(LO2-3, 75 minutes, essential)*
    - The librarian creates new teams with at least one person from each of the four groups during the first session. *(Pre-session and 5 minutes to separate into new groups)*
    - In their teams, students discuss what their solutions and sources from the first session were and how they could apply to the new, multidisciplinary problem. *(LO2, 25 minutes)*
    - On large sheets of paper, each team records their emergency preparedness plan and records any additional sources they needed to consult. If a student is part of a team and was not in the first session, finding additional sources can be delegated to them. *(LO2, 15 minutes)*
    - The teams present their emergency preparedness plans. The other teams are encouraged to ask questions after each presentation. *(LO3, 20 minutes)*
    - At the conclusion, students are asked to identify what they would add, remove, or modify in their team's plan. *(LO3, 10 minutes)*

Classroom Management Scenarios

Best-Case Scenario

Self-directed students take control of their learning and are comfortable working in small groups. Their advanced information literacy skills, which include finding library and open web resources, evaluating information sources, and utilizing those sources, enable them to dive head first into their problems during the first session. They are vocal students willing to collaborate, share their ideas, and maintain an open-minded approach to inquiry. During the second session, the students combine their research, ask new and relevant questions about the problem, and synthesize their solutions in a coherent plan.

Worst-Case Scenario

Uncooperative students are unmotivated and cannot function in small groups. They require more library instruction than anticipated or lack the skills to locate relevant information sources. One or more groups misinterpret the prompt and lose time working toward an incorrect goal. Some students did not attend the first session and are lost or unable to understand the purpose of the second session because they lack context. Students fail to maintain an open mind and do not adjust their viewpoints when approaching the problem from a multidisciplinary angle during the second session.

Possible Solutions

For students unaccustomed to working in small groups, consider creating a step-by-step worksheet that outlines the brainstorming and research process. In the second session, plan for time to recap the first session for students who were absent. While librarians cannot make students maintain an open mind, take note of those students who exhibit engaged behaviors in the first session. When forming groups, these students may be used as anchors for their more reluctant classmates.

Assessment

Assessment Goals

Because the University Scholars Institute focuses on multidisciplinary collaboration, we created assessments that capture students' open-mindedness to multidisciplinary approaches. Additionally, we want to determine whether students provide evidence of incorporating sources from multiple disciplines.

Assessment Tools

Session One

During the first session, students receive a handout with their scenarios (as described above), which includes instructions to cite two sources to justify their decisions, plans, etc. These handouts are collected by the instructors and used as assessment pieces using this simple checklist:

	Relevant to the scenario	Links the source to the applicable portion of their scenario	Sufficient citation information to locate the source	Source is unique from group members' sources
Source 1				
Source 2				
Addition Source (if applicable)				
Addition Source (if applicable)				

This assessment also proves helpful when determining groups for the second session. We want to ensure that each new group completes enough research to be successful during the second session activities.

Session Two

In the second session, we are most interested in how and if students' collaboration represents a multidisciplinary approach. While this is difficult to gauge in a seventy-five-minute session, their emergency plans provide insight into this. We collect the teams' emergency plans created during the second session. In combination with the group members' handouts from the first session, these plans provide insight into whether or not students integrate multiple sources reflecting diverse disciplinary perspectives. The assessment is a simple rubric which accounts for all four perspectives from the first session being represented in the final emergency plan.

	4	3	2	1
Team Emergency Preparedness Plans	All four groups' perspectives represented* in the final emergency plan	Three of the four groups' perspectives represented in the final emergency plan	Two of the four groups' perspectives represented in the final emergency plan	One of the four groups' perspectives represented in the final emergency plan

*If all four perspectives are not present in the final emergency plan, a rationale (verbal or written) as to why one or more is excluded should count as adequate representation.

Notes

1. Mark A. Albanese and Susan Mitchell, "Problem-Based Learning: A Review of Literature on Its Outcomes and Implication Issues," *Academic Medicine: Journal of the Association of American Medical Colleges* 68, no. 1 (1993): 52–81.
2. V. R. Neufeld, C. A. Woodward, and S. M. Macleod, "The McMaster M.D. Program: A Case Study of Renewal in Medical Education," *Academic Medicine: Journal of the Association of American Medical Colleges* 64, no. 8 (1989): 423–32.
3. Association of College and Research Libraries, *Framework for Information Literacy for Higher Education*, text (February 9, 2015), http://www.ala.org/acrl/standards/ilframework.
4. Ibid.
5. Ibid.
6. Ibid.

Bibliography

Albanese, Mark A., and Susan Mitchell. "Problem-Based Learning: A Review of Literature on Its Outcomes and Implication Issues." *Academic Medicine: Journal of the Association of American Medical Colleges* 68, no. 1 (1993): 52–81.

Association of College & Research Libraries. *Framework for Information Literacy for Higher Education*. February 2, 2015. http://www.ala.org/acrl/standards/ilframework.

Neufeld, V. R., C. A. Woodward, and S. M. Macleod. "The McMaster M.D. Program: A Case Study of Renewal in Medical Education." *Academic Medicine: Journal of the Association of American Medical Colleges* 64, no. 8 (1989): 423–32.

CHAPTER 9

Know What You Don't Know:

Teaching Chemistry Students to Ask Better Research Questions

Talitha R. Matlin
STEM Librarian
California State University, San Marcos

Michael Schmidt
Professor of Chemistry
California State University, San Marcos

ACRL Information Literacy Frame: Research as Inquiry
Discipline: Science & Engineering
Subject: Chemistry
Learning Theory: Constructivism
Instructional Strategy: Threshold Concepts
Special Population: Undergraduate Students

At California State University, San Marcos (CSUSM),[1] teaching librarians work closely with disciplinary faculty to both develop and deliver information literacy instruction for students in their majors. Oftentimes, this results in long-term partnerships of individual librarians and teaching faculty to rethink and reimagine what information literacy instruction looks like in the classroom. As the STEM librarian, I (T. R. M.) have worked closely with a professor in the Chemistry department (M. S.) on an upper-division course called The Literature of Chemistry (Chem 300). Chem 300 is a required course for chemistry and biochemistry majors in which they are introduced to the techniques of finding, reading, and writing chemical literature. The centerpiece project is a home chemistry experiment, which requires students to proceed step-by-step through the research process. If I had to describe the main learning objective of Chem 300, it would be "learn how to find, read, and use information like a chemist—and why."

For the last four years, I have been responsible for four sessions (amounting to two weeks in a sixteen-week semester) that cover the broad topics of books, journals, citations and bibliographic managers, and Web of Science. These sessions each include a lecture component, in-class activities, and homework assignments that I am responsible for grading. This past year, the professor came to me before the semester to discuss some possible changes to the content of each of the lessons. In previous semesters, the professor had done an assignment early in the semester to get students looking at general reference works, typically encyclopedias and online references,[2] to get some background information for their project proposals. Although the lesson was focused on the usefulness of these reference works, it was often the case that the most useful information for the students at this stage of their research was not in these works but on the open web. I would give a lesson later in the semester on books and the library catalog, which, while ensuring that students had basic information on these topics, did not always result in students advancing their research project. This exercise ended up feeling inauthentic because many times we would tell them to find a book that was only tangentially related to their research topic just so they could complete the assignment. Students felt frustrated that, in both of these lessons, the in-class work and homework assignments required them to focus their background research on print sources. We decided to abandon the general reference works lesson and hand over that day in the schedule to me to do a more general introduction to finding information. In light of the new ACRL *Framework for Information Literacy for Higher Education*,[3] this gave me an opportunity to rethink the way Chem 300 students embarked on research for their projects.

ACRL Information Literacy Frame: Research as Inquiry

During our initial planning meeting prior to the start of the semester, I asked the professor what he wanted students to understand and to be able to do after the session. He told me that he mainly wanted students to get the information they needed to ask better questions in order to drive their research—a goal that matched up perfectly with the ACRL frame Research as Inquiry, which states, "Research is iterative and depends upon asking increasingly complex or new questions whose answers in turn develop additional questions or lines of inquiry in any field."[4] At the core of the lesson, we want students to be able to articulate what they did not yet know and/or understand, formulate questions based on their lack of knowledge and understanding, and try to think about where they would go next to learn the answers to their questions.

Learning Theory: Constructivism

The revised lesson plan draws upon a learning theory and an instructional strategy—constructivism and threshold concepts. In constructivism (a concept which appears extensively in the library instruction literature), the focus is on engaging "students …with information to solve a problem and thereby creating new understanding through *active* investigation and thought, instead of memorizing facts presented in class lectures."[5] The key word here is "active"; rather than the librarian/professor "transmitting" information to the student, students construct knowledge "through the process of trying to make sense of new information in terms of what that individual already knows."[6] In our lesson, students start with their preliminary ideas for "at home" research; this is what they already know. However, they are lacking an understanding of how to take these preliminary ideas and turn them into workable research questions. A lecture-based lesson that tells students how to arrive at better questions would not provide students with the vital practice of actual inquiry.

In the revised lesson, much of the lecture portion (which included information on the difference between primary/secondary/tertiary sources, how to find books using library classification systems, and a demonstration of how to use various book catalogs) is shifted to pre-class reading on some of these topics prepared by the professor. Although there is still a short lecture at the beginning of the session, most of it focuses on the purpose of background information and the different places students might go to learn what they need to know and how this would drive their research process. They are then provided with a large amount of in-class time to complete a worksheet[7] that walks them through the background research as question development process. Students thus construct their own knowledge both of their research topics and the inquiry process through the activities of the lesson.

This worksheet asks students to

- articulate their research interests;
- learn more about their topic by consulting a variety of sources;
- write down vocabulary terms and definitions, as well as where they found the terms;
- articulate new questions that occur to them while conducting background research and think about where they might look for the answer;
- determine what their "observables" will be in their experimental research project (the project requires quantitative data, and the students often have a hard time specifying just what parameters will be measured; background research can be useful in clarifying this for them);
- write down two new sources they encounter during their background research that they might want to find and consult; and
- locate one book that might be useful for their research.

In creating the worksheet, I found it extremely helpful to consult the ACRL frame Research as Inquiry and its knowledge practices that state, "Learners who are developing their information literate abilities formulate questions for research based on information gaps or on reexamination of existing, possibly conflicting, information" and "... deal with complex research by breaking complex questions into simple ones, limiting the scope of investigations."[8] This worksheet helped students to do all of these things: take a seemingly large research topic, determine what they do not yet know, and ask simpler questions that will ultimately help them develop and answer their "big" question.

Instructional Strategy: Threshold Concepts

In addition to constructivism, this lesson is also based on the instructional strategy threshold concepts. In their extensive writing on the subject, Meyer and Land have described threshold concepts as transformative, irreversible, integrative, bounded, and possibly troublesome, and as concepts which "...can be considered as akin to a portal, opening up a new and previously inaccessible way of thinking about something."[9] Talanquer considers the idea of threshold concepts within the field of chemistry, stating that threshold concepts are, "…in very general terms, the types of disciplinary practices that learners have to master to comprehend how knowledge is established …within a discipline."[10] As stated previously, the informal learning objective of Chem 300 is that students will "learn how to find, read, and use information like a chemist—and why." The threshold concept we want students to understand after this lesson is how chemists conduct background research as their first step in the research process. Not only will students need to research and learn about fundamental chemistry concepts, they will also need to gain an understanding of the scope and breadth of sources in which they can learn about these chemistry concepts.

In prior semesters, the professor and I had seen students struggle when conducting their background research—they always wanted to jump right into primary research articles before they understood much (if anything) about their proposed research topic. Based on observed student reactions, it seemed that the students considered non-scholarly web sources as antithetical (and "troublesome") to their preconceived notions of what scientists do. This attitude may be reinforced in other classes where the professor specifies that a project must ultimately be based on peer-reviewed scholarly articles—while failing to mention that the student must often do more basic background research to understand these sources. The new lesson plan emphasizes the importance of "approaching a high peak by choosing the gentle slope"[11]—basically, start by learning the easy concepts first before progressing to the harder stuff. The first time I taught this lesson, one of the students told me she was worried she was not able to find any scholarly articles that included an anatomical diagram of the human eye, so I asked her what kind of source might have the information she was looking for. She said, "Well, I know that I can go to places like Wikipedia or Khan Academy, but those aren't good." When I told her that those kinds of sources were indeed "good enough" for this kind of information and that it was likely she would not even be able to find them in the more specific scholarly articles, I saw a light bulb go off for her—she was crossing the threshold. Although for professional chemists, the background research they have to conduct starts at a more advanced level, the concept remains the same: first, learn about what you do not know before trying to understand more difficult information. And for students, understanding this concept transforms how they conduct research.

The previously described anecdote, in which the student comes to the realization about how to best address the gaps in their knowledge, is the "best case" scenario. By figuring out what she did not yet understand and then locating answers to her basic questions, she was then able to ask more sophisticated (and relevant) questions that drove her research.

This past semester, the "worst cases" tended to fall into two different categories, both of which were related to the question portion of the in-class assignment. In the first category, students asked questions that were too advanced or complicated during the background research portion of the in-class work because, at this point, they did not have the background knowledge necessary to ask appropriate questions. An example of a question that is too complex at this point would be "What are the effects of sulfate-free shampoo on color-treated hair?" as the student first needs to ask something more fundamental like "How do shampoos and dyes interact?" or even "How does shampoo work?" In the second category, students continued to ask very closed-ended questions that did not get them any closer to good experimental questions. Although closed-ended questions are not necessarily inappropriate to ask at this point in their research process, students were not conducting true inquiry in which their questions became more and more nuanced/complex; instead, it was more like they were "spinning their wheels" and not progressing in their research. An example of this "worst case" would be a student starting out with a research topic of the effect of different yeast types on the hardness of bread. Questions like "What are different types of yeast?" and "What types of bread are there?" are closed-ended, while questions like "What is the function of yeast in baking bread?" or "What do I mean by hardness and how do I measure it?" could yield further insights and improve their experimental research plans.

According to the American Chemical Society's *Guidelines and Evaluation Procedures for Bachelor's Degree Programs*, students graduating from an undergraduate chemistry program should be able to "…retrieve information efficiently and effectively by searching the chemical literature…" and they "…must be instructed in effective methods for performing and assessing the quality of searches using keywords, authors, abstracts, citations, patents, and structures/substructures…."[12] The professor and I do provide such instruction for students enrolled in Chem 300: The Literature of Chemistry; however, before they are prepared to engage in this level of research, we first try to set them up with a good solid foundation in question formulation and background research.

Although this lesson has only been used in a chemistry class, it could be adapted to work for any subject. The process of articulating unknowns, determining where to learn the answers, and asking more advanced questions is the core of the ACRL frame Research as Inquiry and can be applied to any discipline. Certain aspects of the in-class activity (such as the requirement for noting down "observables"[13]) would need to be modified for non-experimental situations.

Lesson Plan

Learner Analysis

- This lesson is appropriate for an upper-level undergraduate chemistry or biochemistry major (although it could easily be modified for many different student populations). Learners should have completed their lower-division chemistry coursework, including general chemistry, organic chemistry, physical chemistry, and quantitative chemistry.
- This lesson will work best with students who are ready to undertake a semester-long research project with the professor's guidance. Students should have basic disciplinary knowledge (including general laboratory techniques) that will allow them to articulate a research topic of interest and design and execute a simple home chemistry experiment.

Orienting Context and Prerequisites

Prior to the lesson, students should have:

- identified a potential area of research; and
- completed the reading[14] overviewing the different types of literature (primary, secondary, tertiary), library classification schemes, and a general overview of how experts in the field conduct research/inquiry.

Instructional Context

- At the very least, the classroom should provide internet access for each student. Ideally, the class should be held in the library to provide easy access to print reference works relevant to the course topic. Seventy-five minutes to an hour and a half is the ideal length for this lesson, although it can be completed in fifty minutes if much of the in-class activity is shifted to homework. Prior to delivering the lesson, the librarian should develop the in-class activity and either bring printouts to class for the students to complete or post an electronic copy of the handout online for students to fill out on their computers.

Learning Outcomes and Activities

Learning Outcomes

After the lesson, students will:

1. know how to begin conducting background research on a topic;
2. know the type of information they can find in books and online;
3. be able to ask appropriate questions to drive their background research;
4. be able to access and log in to the library website in order to access proprietary materials;
5. be able to search the library catalog to find books by keyword and subject; and
6. be able to request items through interlibrary loan.

Learning Activities

1. Lecture: Students learn about the research process, the purpose of background research, and searching in library catalogs. *(LO1-6, 30 minutes, essential)*
    a. What are we covering today? (*LO1*)
        i. How to begin conducting background research
        ii. Search strategies (catalog)
        iii. Different library catalogs
        iv. Worksheet—find a book/books on your research topic, begin keeping track of important vocabulary, find similar experiments that have been done online, keep track of questions you are starting to have
    b. Basic intro to library website *(LO4-6)*
        i. How to log in, access materials off-site, the type of materials held in the library (physical and electronic), how to get help from a librarian

c. Beginning your background research—*research as inquiry (LO2)*
    i. Your information need is contextual; the type of source you want to seek out and the kind of information that is useful to you will depend on where you are in your research. At this point, what is your information need and where do you think is the best place to find this information?
    ii. Utility of books in conducting background research
        1. What kind of books have you used in the past?
        2. What *is* a book, exactly? What are they good for?
        3. Brief overview of how books are organized (Library of Congress classification and subject headings)
        4. Tools for finding books (catalogs, interlibrary loan)
    iii. Conducting background research
        1. You've already started thinking about your research questions/possible experiments, but what is your research need *now*, and where will you go to learn more?
            a. Open web and book
            b. Type of info you're looking for:
                i. Vocab and definitions
                ii. What has been done before
            c. What you need to produce:
                i. Questions you have that will drive your research forward
                ii. List of observables
                iii. List of sources for further investigation

2. Worksheet: Students begin their background research and articulate the following questions and unknowns *(LO3, 45 minutes, essential)*

a. In a couple of sentences, write out your possible area of research for your home chemistry assignment.
b. Begin your background research. You may want to visit websites, consult library books, look through book records in the library catalog, and more.
c. Vocabulary. Use this space to note down at least five relevant vocabulary terms, brief definitions, and where you found them.
d. New questions. Use this space to jot down at least four questions that occur to you during your background research that you will need to answer in order to continue on your home chemistry experiment. Write down where you might go to learn the answer.
e. Observables. In doing your home chemistry experiment, what will you need to observe and quantify in order to gather useful data?
f. Other references. In your background research, you will come across citations and/or links to other potentially useful sources. Use this space to write down at least two other sources you will want to investigate further.
g. Find one book (either in our library's collection or interlibrary loan) that might be useful for your research. Write out the **title**, **call number**, and any relevant **subject headings**.

Assessment

Summative Assessment

Following a rubric, the librarian assesses student worksheets and their demonstration of discrete skills (such as the ability to locate a book through the library's catalog) and the following knowledge practices, which state:

- "Learners who are developing their information literate abilities:
    - ▷ formulate questions for research based on information gaps or on reexamination of existing, possibly conflicting, information;
    - ▷ deal with complex research by breaking complex questions into simple ones, limiting the scope of investigations; and

- ▷ use various research methods, based on need, circumstance, and type of inquiry."[15]

Formative Assessment

Throughout the lesson, both the librarian and the professor are available to assist students with their question formulation and source selection.

- Success is measured by student achievement of the learning outcomes. By the end of the lesson, students should have a clearer direction for the necessary steps they should take to progress in their research and should have articulated more complex questions that can possibly be answered through experimentation.

Notes

1. CSUSM is one of twenty-three campuses in the California State University system and has a student population of approximately 14,000. "Fast Facts," CSUSM, accessed September 28, 2016.
2. The classification of "general reference works," while not used by librarians, was preferred by the professor to distinguish works written for a more general scientific audience from those reference works that primarily contained chemical or physical data, which he called "technical reference works."
3. Association of College & Research Libraries, *Framework for Information Literacy for Higher Education*, accessed September 28, 2016, http://www.ala.org/acrl/standards/ilframework.
4. Ibid.
5. Jesús Lau, "Guidelines on Information Literacy for Lifelong Learning," IFLA, 9 (my italics).
6. Alison King, "From Sage on the Stage to Guide on the Side," JSTOR, 6.
7. Talitha Matlin and Michael Schmidt, "Chem 300 Background Research Assignment," California State University San Marcos (see Learning Outcomes and Activities).
8. Association of College & Research Libraries, "Framework."
9. Jan Meyer and Ray Land, "Threshold Concepts and Troublesome Knowledge: Linkages to Ways of Thinking and Practising within the Disciplines," occasional report, Enhancing Teaching-Learning Environments in Undergraduate Courses Project, Edinburgh: School of Education, University of Edinburgh, May 2003, https://kennslumidstod.hi.is/wp-content/uploads/2016/04/meyerandland.pdf, 1.
10. Vicente Talanquer, "Threshold Concepts in Chemistry: The Critical Role of Implicit Schemas," *Journal of Chemical Education* 92, no. 1 (January 13, 2015): 3–9, doi:10.1021/ed500679k.
11. This analogy comes from the unpublished text for Chemistry 300, written by Dr. Michael Schmidt.
12. American Chemical Society, "Undergraduate Professional Education in Chemistry: ACS Guidelines and Evaluation Procedures for Bachelor's Degree Programs," 16–17.
13. Matlin and Schmidt, "Chem 300" (see Learning Outcomes and Activities).
14. Unpublished text for Chemistry 300, written by Dr. Michael Schmidt.
15. Association of College & Research Libraries, "Framework."

Bibliography

American Chemical Society. "Undergraduate Professional Education in Chemistry: ACS Guidelines and Evaluation Procedures for Bachelor's Degree Programs." ACS (2015). https://www.acs.org/content/dam/acsorg/about/governance/committees/training/2015-acs-guidelines-for-bachelors-degree-programs.pdf.

Association of College & Research Libraries. *Framework for Information Literacy for Higher Education*. Text (2016). http://www.ala.org/acrl/standards/ilframework.

Cooperstein, Susan E., and Elizabeth Kocevar-Weidinger. "Beyond Active Learning: A Constructivist Approach to Learning." *Reference Services Review* 32, no. 2 (June 2004): 141–48. doi:10.1108/00907320410537658.

CSUSM. "Fast Facts." *Fast Facts*. 2015. http://news.csusm.edu/fast-facts.

King, Alison. "From Sage on the Stage to Guide on the Side." *College Teaching* 41, no. 1 (1993): 30–35.

Lau, Jesús. "IFLA—Guidelines on Information Literacy for Lifelong Learning." Accessed September 29, 2016. http://www.ifla.org/publications/guidelines-on-information-literacy-for-lifelong-learning.

Matlin, Talitha R., and Michael Schmidt. "Chem 300 Background Research Assignment." CSU San Marcos (2016).

Meyer, Jan, and Ray Land. "Threshold Concepts and Troublesome Knowledge: Linkages to Ways of Thinking and Practising within the Disciplines." Occasional report. Enhancing Teaching-Learning Environments in Undergraduate Courses Project. Edinburgh: School of Education, University of Edinburgh. May 2003. https://kennslumidstod.hi.is/wp-content/uploads/2016/04/meyerandland.pdf.

Talanquer, Vicente. "Threshold Concepts in Chemistry: The Critical Role of Implicit Schemas." *Journal of Chemical Education* 92, no. 1 (January 13, 2015): 3–9. doi:10.1021/ed500679k.

CHAPTER 10

Empowering Undergraduates in the Life Sciences with Information Literacy Skills for Graduate Research Readiness

Kelli Trei
Biosciences Librarian & Assistant Professor
University of Illinois at Urbana-Champaign

ACRL Information Literacy Frame: Research as Inquiry
Discipline: Science & Engineering
Subject: Biosciences
Learning Theory: Cognitive Constructivism
Special Population: Undergraduate Students

This chapter details a lesson plan co-created by life science librarians and a professor in the sciences at the University of Illinois at Urbana-Champaign to teach information literacy skills to junior and senior undergraduates. The class period, entitled "Mastering the Scientific Literature," uses cognitive constructivism theory to support the theme "Research as Inquiry" in the

ACRL *Framework for Information Literacy for Higher Education*[1] in order to prepare the students as they prepare to conduct graduate-level research. The faculty member who initiated this class instruction teaches this elective class for undergraduate students in the life sciences who wish to attend graduate college. The initial iteration of the pre-class homework assignment was conceived by the needs identified by the professor and, in 2013, the first class period was planned with the librarian. From the professor's personal experience with new graduate students, she identified a need for the students to be fully aware of what it meant to create a research strategy and begin to investigate their research ideas. They must identify literature related to their field of study in order to identify gaps in the existing literature and develop their own research plan. They must be able to find resources, identify those most useful, and parse through them to find the specific information they seek.

Learning Theory: Cognitive Constructivism

This lesson plan is based in the learning theory, cognitive constructivism. Cognitive constructivism is a conglomeration of theories historically developed by John Dewey, Jean Piaget, Lev Vygotsky, and Jerome Bruner. However, there is much debate and discussion about the varying ways these theories can be applied to instruction, although most agree the theory is concerned with how knowledge is actively created in the mind.[2] More a learning theory than a teaching theory, an article in the *International Journal of Science Education* established four criteria to use when designing a lesson using cognitive constructivism: eliciting prior knowledge, creating cognitive dissonance, application of new knowledge with feedback, and reflection on learning.[3] Our plan uses the four criteria in these ways:

1. Eliciting prior knowledge. This criterion is met with the use of a pre-assignment to gauge what the student already knows and how they apply that knowledge to specific questions.
2. Creating cognitive dissonance. This criterion is met by challenging the ideas the students have from their pre-assignment and highlighting new and better options during the presentations and class discussion.
3. Application of new knowledge with feedback. This criterion is met when we discuss the problems students may have had in each sec-

tion of their assignment and, with the instructor, librarian, and peer feedback, we conduct example searches to solve those issues with our newly developed skills.

4. Reflection on learning. This criterion is met when the students revise the pre-assignment and submit it having applied the new information they have learned to the questions.

ACRL Information Literacy Frame: Research as Inquiry

The new ACRL Framework "Research as Inquiry" section highlights the importance of the iterative process of learning.[4] It also highlights the importance of dialogue and debate to determine the best ways to identify material. It focuses on determining the appropriate scope for research, continuously fine-tuning that scope, critically evaluating information and tools, and drawing conclusions. Our class assignment and class discussion will encourage those framework components that include the explorative process of research, the need to be flexible, persistent, and ask for help when needed, and to recognize our own limitations.

The pre-class assignment from the instructor asks the students to think about what graduate research they might like to do and formulate research questions around that idea. They are then asked to identify terms they would use to search, databases they would use, and how they would store this information for future use (Appendix 10A). As these students are electively taking this class to prepare for a graduate-level research position, they have already been thinking about their research interests and ideas. They will also have discussed the idea of a research plan more broadly with the instructor beforehand. The prior knowledge of databases on campus will be familiar to the students from other projects in school, and those who prefer Google Scholar to campus databases will learn the strengths and weaknesses of that tool as well. This session seeks to capitalize on the specific knowledge these students need to succeed and how to evaluate resources to meet those specific needs, using the institution's resources as examples.

The librarian reviews the student submissions before their instruction period in order to personalize the session (e.g., choosing appropriate databases to discuss), adding feedback to the assignment which is returned to the students after in-class discussion. It is important that the students come to class having approached the questions with the information they already have, both so they do not try to give "correct answers" and so the instructor and librarian can learn about the initial approach each student takes and refine the lesson. Moreover, the student has ownership of their plan from the beginning and will formulate questions and searches it in a way that is personally relevant. This would not be achievable in a one-hour class session on an individual level, so these assignments are key. The students' assignments are finalized when they incorporate the elements of class discussion and feedback and submit a revised version of the pre-assignment to their instructor. They only receive full credit for the assignment if they have made these changes. In this class, the assignment is treated as pass/fail and students only received credit if they completed the work in its entirety.

We revised the library lesson plan over time, taking student needs and feedback into consideration. Initially, we included additional skills in the session, such as creating RSS feeds, constructing advanced search strings in specific databases, and defining peer-review in publishing. Teaching all of these skills took too much of the time allowed and taxed the attention span of the class. We revised the session to allow for the databases we discussed to vary, depending on each particular group of students. Broad scientific publishing ideas like peer-review and primary versus secondary literature are covered in a previous session with the instructor so the librarian can concentrate on Boolean searching skills that can be used in every database. In this way, the class is able to have a broader discussion of critically evaluating resources to identify the most beneficial database for each research question.

In an optimal class session, two to three students will give a brief presentation of their assignment, including what worked well and what did not. The presentation is informal, they may use slides or just talk about what they did. We typically ask for volunteers, and the low-key nature of their presentation makes students more willing to share. The librarian may then begin to ask questions related to the difficulties the students faced in their work and start the comparison and demonstration of databases based on the examples they pull from this presentation. We ask the presenting students as well as the class to suggest alternative databases or search terms as we proceed through the demonstration to establish a more iterative flow of ideas. We guide the students by pointing out what works better as far as Boolean search terms and limiters in the databases. We further synthesize this process by using scientific language discovered in article abstracts to create more precise search results.

As we look at more databases during the session, we ask the students again for ideas and we continue to apply the same elements using different resources. Research as Inquiry shapes this process as the librarian may use student feedback to demonstrate a move from broad databases, like Google Scholar, to more specific resources, such as PubMed. We critically evaluate particular strengths of certain databases compared to others. Exhibiting the use of limiters and other database-specific tools helps the students break complex questions into more simple ones. As experimental scientific research is generally built around the questioning of commonly held assertions as well as testing those assertions through new research ideas, the session compliments that process by adjusting the search strategy based on the quality of the information discovered. If students come unprepared or no one presents their findings, the librarian will use the same questions from the assignment to begin the discussion and build a search demonstration around specific ideas. As this assignment is instructor-driven, and the class is an elective for students with a particular desire to conduct research, most assignments are thoughtfully completed.

This class period embraces the iterative nature of both cognitive constructivism and the ACRL Research as Inquiry frame. The students begin the process with their prior knowledge, receive feedback from both a library science perspective as well as a critical science perspective, and learn new techniques from the librarian throughout this investigation. Since the students have individual ownership of the research questions they hypothesized before class begins, they are invested in the tools they learn to make their research even more effective. This class encourages individual exploration in the scientific literature by equipping students with the tools to critically refine a search to achieve accurate and useful information to strengthen their research plan. The class enables information-literate undergraduate students to use their skills to effectively propose a research plan to graduate programs and prepares them for success in conducting graduate-level research.

Lesson Plan

Learner Analysis

The typical students are junior or senior undergraduates who intend on pursuing graduate studies.

Limitations

- A student unfamiliar with the library website may have difficulty following along.
- This project works best in classes of fifteen students or fewer.

Opportunities

- The students with aspirations for graduate-level research will benefit most from this session as it requires significant self-motivation in thoughtfully identifying a research question of interest.

Orienting Context and Prerequisites

Pre-instruction learner tasks

- The students will complete an assignment before class with the following questions (see Appendix 10A, *essential*):

1. Name your desired discipline of study.
    a. List the specific sub-disciplines, if they exist.
    b. List the targeted subject areas.
2. List specific research questions you would ask in this subject area.
3. List the search terms you used for investigation into your research questions.
4. List where you looked for literature using these search terms.
5. Explain how and where you would save the literature you found for future use.
    - The students will submit this assignment to the instructor at least one week before class period.
    - Two to three students must prepare to discuss the results of the pre-learner assignment with the class (optimal).

Learner prerequisites

- The student must be familiar with the library website.

Instructional Context

Technology Needs (optimal)

- projection screen with computer connection or hookup for laptop
- wireless internet
- laptops or computers for every student

Technology Needs (essential)

- projection screen with hookup for laptop
- wireless internet

Instructor Preparation

- The instructor will share the assignment submissions with the librarian at least three days before the class period.
- The librarian will review each student's submission and add feedback to the assignments before the class period.
- The librarian will create a handout to pass out or email after class with the following information:
    1. contact information and availability
    2. relevant workshop information (for example, dates of citation management workshops)
    3. any other information the librarian thinks would be useful
- The librarian will create an anonymous comment sheet to pass out after class.

Learning Outcomes and Activities

Learning Outcomes

1. The student will be able to identify the major databases in the scientific fields.
2. The student will be able to identify the limitations of these databases.
3. The student will be able to construct basic Boolean search strings.
4. The student will be able to conduct an iterative search.
5. The student will be able to identify options for storing and organize literature for future use.

Learning Activities

Pre-Class Assignment *(essential)*

1. Students will complete a pre-class assignment (see Appendix 10A) as detailed in pre-instruction learner tasks.

Option 1: In-Class with Student Presentations *(55 minutes)*

1. Student Presentations *(10–15 minutes, 5 minutes each)*

- Two or three students will individually present their findings from the pre-assignment to the class (optional, but highly encouraged).
    - ▷ When presentations are included, the librarian will use them as examples throughout, drawing on what the students felt worked and what was more difficult.

2. Demonstrate and discuss up to three databases specific to the research interests of the students. *(LO1, 8 minutes, essential)*
    - ▷ The librarian will choose subject-specific databases useful for the research questions the students posed in the pre-assignment.
    - ▷ The databases covered will vary per session based on the librarian's evaluation of the research questions. As an example, in our sessions, the following databases were most frequently discussed: Scopus, Web of Science, and PubMed.
3. Demonstrate and discuss the limitations and strengths of databases selected. *(LO2, 7 minutes, essential)*
    - ▷ Scope of the database
        - ♦ Compare and contrast the general databases students may have identified in their pre-assignment, such as Google Scholar.
    - ▷ General structure of the database
    - ▷ Limiters available in the database
4. Explain Boolean searching. *(LO3, 5 minutes, essential)*
    - ▷ Define the use of AND, OR, NOT, and quotation operators to students.
    - ▷ Ask students for operators to make an example search more narrow.
    - ▷ Ask students for operators to make an example search broader.
5. Demonstrate iterative searching using keywords, database limiters, and Boolean operators. *(LO4, 7 minutes, essential)*
    - ▷ Construct a Boolean search with keywords identified by the students.
    - ▷ In each database, use limiters or keywords to further change the search; for example:

- ♦ adding keywords from initial results in search
- ♦ limiting by:
  - * years
  - * institutions
  - * subjects
  - * type of document

6. Highlight citation management software options for saving and organizing gathered information. *(LO5, 5 minutes, essential)*
   - ▷ Some examples may include EndNote, Mendeley, Zotero, or RefWorks (up to librarian's discretion, institution availability).
   - ▷ Explain the benefits of using these resources.
   - ▷ Give students information to follow up after class, such as:
     - ♦ workshops on campus
     - ♦ websites and resource guide information
7. Provide librarian contact information. *(3 minutes)*
8. Pass out handout and comment sheets. *(5 minutes)*

Option 2: In-Class without Student Presentations *(55 minutes minimal)*

1. The librarian will begin the instruction asking for suggestions of research questions and search terms from the student pre-assignments. *(5 minutes)*
2. Demonstrate and discuss up to three databases specific to the research interests of the students. *(LO1, 10 minutes, essential)*
   - ▷ The librarian will choose subject-specific databases useful for the research questions the students posed in the pre-assignment.
   - ▷ The databases covered will vary per session based on the librarian's evaluation of the research questions. As an example, in our sessions, the following databases were most frequently discussed: Scopus, Web of Science, and PubMed.
3. Demonstrate and discuss the limitations and strengths of databases selected. *(LO2, 8 minutes, essential)*
   - ▷ Scope of the database
     - ♦ Compare and contrast the general databases students may have identified in their pre-assignment, such as Google Scholar.

- ▷ General structure of the database
- ▷ Limiters available in the database

4. Explain Boolean searching. *(LO3, 8 minutes, essential)*
    - ▷ Define the use of AND, OR, NOT, and quotation operators to students.
    - ▷ Ask students for operators to make an example search more narrow.
    - ▷ Ask students for operators to make an example search broader.
5. Demonstrate iterative searching using keywords, database limiters, and Boolean operators. *(LO4, 10 minutes, essential)*
    - ▷ Construct a Boolean search with keywords identified by the students.
    - ▷ In each database, use limiters or keywords to further change the search; for example:
        - ♦ adding keywords from initial results in search
        - ♦ limiting by:
            - * years
            - * institutions
            - * subjects
            - * type of document
6. Highlight citation management software options for saving and organizing gathered information. *(LO5, 6 minutes, essential)*
    - ▷ Some examples may include EndNote, Mendeley, Zotero, or RefWorks (up to librarian's discretion, institution availability).
    - ▷ Explain the benefits of using these resources.
    - ▷ Give students information to follow up after class, such as:
        - ♦ workshops on campus
        - ♦ websites and resource guide information
7. Provide librarian contact information. *(3 minutes)*
8. Pass out handout and comment sheets. *(5 minutes)*

Assessment

Summative Assessment

- Anonymous comment sheets will be circulated at the end of the

class period to the students and instructor with the following questions:
  - What did you learn that you did not already know?
  - What are you still confused about?
  - How could this session have been better?
- Anonymous comment sheets will be collected by the librarian.
  - Comments will be used to shape the session in the future.

Summative assessment of the student work by the instructor:
- The instructor will:
  - return the assignments to the students with the librarian's feedback attached for revisions; and
  - review the student's resubmissions, evaluate them based on incorporation of librarian feedback and class discussion, and return them to the students with any additional comments.

Appendix 10A

Example of Assignment

Answer these questions describing the area of research you would most want to conduct in graduate school. Be as detailed as possible in your responses.

1. Discipline:
   Subdiscipline(s):
   Targeted Subject Areas:
   Specific Research Questions:
2. What search terms will you use?
3. Where will you look?
4. How will you organize your information?

Notes

1. American Library Association, *Framework for Information Literacy for Higher Education*, accessed January 27, 2017, http://www.ala.org/acrl/standards/ilframework.
2. Virginia Richardson, "Constructivist Pedagogy," *Teachers College Record* 105, no. 9 (2003): 1625.
3. Sandhya N. Baviskar, R. Todd Hartle, and Tiffany Whitney, "Essential Criteria to Characterize Constructivist Teaching: Derived from a Review of the Literature and Applied to Five Constructivist-Teaching Method Articles," *International Journal of Science Education* 31, no 4 (2009): 543–54, accessed January 27, 2017, doi: 10.1080/09500690701731121.
4. American Library Association, *Framework*.

Bibliography

American Library Association. *Framework for Information Literacy for Higher Education*. February 2, 2015. http://www.ala.org/acrl/standards/ilframework.

Baviskar, Sandhya N., R. Todd Hartle, and Tiffany Whitney. "Essential Criteria to Characterize Constructivist Teaching: Derived from a Review of the Literature and Applied to Five Constructivist-Teaching Method Articles." *International Journal of Science Education* 31, no. 4 (2009): 541–50. Accessed January 27, 2017. doi: 10.1080/09500690701731121.

Richardson, Virginia. "Constructivist Pedagogy." *Teachers College Record* 105, no. 9 (2003): 1623–40.

Scholarship as Conversation:

Social Learning, Storytelling, and Collaboration

Social Learning

There are two different sets of learners that could be potentially impacted by the material in this book. There are direct learners, the readers of this book who are library (or future) library instructors, and there are indirect learners, future students of the readers of this book. As we were developing the format for the book, we thought about what elements make the most useful and the most engaging learning experiences, called for proposals that incorporated unique and engaging instruction, and incorporated these elements in the chapter template authors followed.

The most impactful learning (and teaching) experiences are usually social and/or experiential in nature. The authors of the chapters in this book have picked their most successful teaching experiences to share here, and most of them include group or individual learning activities that directly relate to something relevant in their students' lives, whether it is an assignment or a topic of personal interest.

We learned so much from each other while collaborating on this book. As we began reading drafts of the chapters, we were pleased that some of the authors were talking to each other in their work. In Chapter 38, McManus nods to Carr's (Chapter 35 and 43) teaching as inspiration for her literature review learning activities. Jenemann (Chapter 37) acknowledges Kirker's (Chapter 28) information cycle learning activity as the backbone for her lesson for dance history students. Kirker also writes about the information cycle, but in the context of a research and writing course for advanced students using an environmental science theme. What is so interesting about these two authors' lessons is that they have used the same basic learning activity but recrafted it to meet entirely different learning outcomes, representing two different frames. We hope our readers too will benefit from the social, collaborative experience this book provides.

Collaboration

Five chapters detail successful collaborative efforts between faculty and teacher librarians and are co-written by the instructional faculty and the librarian. In Chapter 9, Matlin and Schmidt share a redesigned information literacy activity for a chemistry course to improve student understanding of the research process. Hassman and Hassman share the TOPIC teaching module created by faculty and librarians to teach first year students about the research process in Chapter 4. In Chapter 15, Belzowski and Bugajski discuss their partnership to redesign a biotechnology course to include activities that promote scientific IL skills by exploring the Information has Value frame. Carpenter, Losoff, and Kuglitsch, in Chapter 40, share a learning activity they collaborated on to get students to engage with Scholarship as Conversation. In Chapter 52, Quintel, Sloane, and Troelstrup highlight the development of an information literacy session on evaluating the authority of scientific information after receiving a university grant to work with faculty partners to integrate the ACRL Framework into their curriculum. The librarians and faculty members created assignments and instruction that would improve student understanding of the role authority plays in the scientific community.

Storytelling

Conversely, while collaboration usually achieves the best possible learning outcomes, there are other pathways to information literacy instruction success. Cultivating confidence and knowledge are other means of meeting teaching goals. It is also important to consider that many faculty are novices when it comes to information literacy themselves. Speaking a faculty member's "instructional language" may be an unexpected outcome of information literacy sessions and may lead to more collaborative efforts between librarians and teaching faculty. Chapter authors include a wide variety of teaching scenarios, including less than optimal teaching conditions and how to recover from them. But most important, each of these chapters tell a unique story with elements that will probably feel familiar to our readers. When we tell our teaching stories, we offer ourselves and others a deeper understanding of teaching and learning.

A Comma, Not a Period

We hope this book will continue to evolve as teacher librarians construct new meanings from the content and begin to critically examine the ACRL *Framework for Information Literacy for Higher Education.* Instead of adding a final period that a conclusion is meant to do at the end of a book, we have added a comma. The editors and chapter authors offer the readers some questions, answers, and words of encouragement to consider as they experiment with the content in this book.

What is the best teaching advice you have ever received?

Be confident...

> The best teaching advice I ever received, especially for freshmen—you know a lot more than they do about research, so pretty much anything you teach them is more than they knew when they first came in! This takes a lot of the pressure off when you just start teaching.
>
> —*Talitha Matlin, California State University, San Marcos*

> The best advice that I have received is to show enthusiasm in every lesson. If you are not passionate about what you are teaching, the students will not be passionate about learning.
>
> —*Kristi Bugajski, Valparaiso University*

Be authentic...

> Teach so the students will acquire knowledge, and not to show off your own knowledge.
>
> —*Laura Skinner, Piedmont Virginia Community College*

The best teaching advice I have ever received is to be myself when teaching. I've learned over the years that it is best not to leave my quirky personality at the door. And, my silly nature allows students to feel comfortable asking questions about subjects that they may find challenging, such as copyright law.

—Sara Benson, University of Illinois

There are different types of teachers in this world. Finding your teaching style is just like finding students' learning styles. Many more of us can teach better than think we can, we just have to find the style that fits. Same goes with learning.

—Laura Jenemann, Boston University

Be yourself and be able to laugh at yourself. Laughter is the best way to break through my "I'm the teacher" mentality where I strive to show students how smart I am, how perfect I am, or what a good teacher I am. Once I let my guard down and let them see the real me, then they can be themselves, ask questions, talk, discuss, learn, and laugh!

—Candace Vance, Murray State University

Be clear…

I was taught, early in my teaching career, how to break my lessons down in ways that made it easier for students to "digest" so to speak. Dealing with one concept at a time before expecting students to deal with concepts in combination, giving students time to practice before moving on to the next thing…it seems to help with retention of ideas in particular.

—Beth Twomey, North Dakota State University

In my classroom management course, I learned that (1) making expectations clear, (2) modeling, and (3) providing opportunities to practice new skills were the Holy Trinity of teaching. It's a lesson that has stood the test of time—or at least the test of my own experience.

—Victoria Elmwood, Loyola University of New Orleans

Be a student advocate...

Don't fear silence or rush to fill it with more lecturing. Those few beats of silence invite thoughtful students to ask more complex questions and shy students to contribute to discussion. A bit of quiet in the classroom is much more effective than "Any questions?"

—Anne Leonard, New York City College of Technology

The best teaching advice I received is to listen to students and to always treat students with respect, and to realize that being culturally literate is essential in teaching students from diverse backgrounds. Students can be the best teachers!

—Sharon Radcliff, California State University, East Bay

As a student, one of us was advised, "Be the difference." We like that advice for teaching, too. It's what we do with and for others that counts.

—Laura Brady and Kelly Diamond, West Virginia University

I often remind myself that it is a privilege and a responsibility to be the person a student comes to when they need help. I can dramatically impact their education and maybe even their world view within a few seconds. Plan accordingly.

—Yvonne Nalani Meulemans, California State University, San Marcos

My Teaching Methods professor told us that teachers make thousands of decisions each day during the course of their lessons, and each of those can impact each student differently. So decide wisely, choose your words and plan your lessons carefully, because all teachers have a role in shaping the lives and futures of their students, and that's not a responsibility to be taken lightly.

—Anna Mary Williford, University of Montevallo

Focus on teaching people first and the content second.

—Charissa Jefferson, California State University, Northridge

Be creative...

Be creative, think outside of the box, students have many different learning styles and there is no one way to do everything.

—Kelli Trei, University of Illinois at Urbana Champaign

Teaching is both science and art. There are proven techniques that enhance students' ability to learn, but creativity is often required in the application of those techniques in the moment.

—Maglen Epstein, St. Olaf College

Be practical...

Teaching is a muscle. It takes practice, time, and patience to strengthen. Don't forget to stretch!

—Maoria Kirker, George Mason University

My sister told me to start by asking myself this question: what do you want the students to be able to do? The answer to that question will become your learning objectives. Then design a lesson plan (or syllabus) that teaches to those objectives.

—Helen McManus, George Mason University

How did you start with learning/teaching theory and why do you feel it is important?

On the job…

I started with problem-based learning because it was the first pedagogy introduced to me as a professional. I quickly realized how impactful it is on student learning to be able to put knowledge and context together. Learning about and incorporating teaching and learning theory has made me a more confident teacher.

—Janna Mattson, George Mason University

When I was in library school there wasn't a course available about instruction or teaching (I'm guessing this was quite common in the late 1990s, though). Although I knew that teaching was what I wanted to do, I didn't realize that it would be a good idea for me to find another way to formally learn about pedagogy and learning theories. Later in my library career I was told that I was a constructivist teacher. After looking this up (embarrassed because I didn't know what it meant) I was happy to find that it matched pretty well with the way that I had been approaching teaching. Reading about the theory (and other theories, eventually) helped me think more deeply about my own teaching and how I might improve it. I think that just knowing that there was a theory behind my practice helped make me a more confident teacher as well.

—Allison Faix, Coastal Carolina University

I came to librarianship after many years working in a trade so when I began teaching information literacy, I was always focused on the question of what I wanted my student to be able to do after I worked with them. I quickly found that constructivist approaches were a good match for what I wanted to accomplish in the classroom. Working consciously and deliberately with pedagogical theory makes you think carefully about each move you and your students make. This has made my teaching much more intentional and effective.

—Beth Twomey, North Dakota State University

There are lots of fads in teaching theory, so in many cases I'm skeptical. Research that describes the development and functioning of human cognition and social behavior has been most helpful for my own instructional design. But folk wisdom passed from teacher to teacher is also crucial to good teaching—it is, first and foremost, a humane profession.

—Victoria Elmwood, Loyola University of New Orleans

In the formal classroom...

I started when I took a two-year course that prepared me for teaching English composition. Over the years, more professional development, including a degree in curriculum design (with a focus on pedagogy), have added useful tools to my toolkit. Learning/teaching theory is crucial if we want to be the best instructors we can possibly be.

—Laura Skinner, Piedmont Virginia Community College

I took a library course in instruction and it was one of the top two most useful classes I completed. I learned about learning theories, different types of learners, and practical skills like creating lesson plans. Even if we do not teach structured instruction sessions, traditional or non-traditional opportunities to teach deserve the mindfulness that comes with instruction education.

—Kelli Trei, University of Illinois at Urbana Champaign

I got a master's degree in English Composition and learning theory was pretty thoroughly integrated into the program, with social constructivism probably receiving the greatest emphasis. A few years later, while working as an academic librarian, I returned to school to work on a doctorate in education in learning and instruction, which focuses on learning theory, and I have taught professional development courses in it to librarians. I think a solid grounding in learning theory, though not essential to being a good teacher, can help!

—Sharon Radcliff, California State University, East Bay

I studied learning and teaching in a Master of Education program soon after graduating college. I gained knowledge and vocabulary for techniques I had seen used and had used myself in various teaching and tutoring sessions. I cannot unlearn what I know about teaching and am grateful for opportunities to transfer my knowledge to my new career in librarianship.

—Maglen Epstein, St. Olaf College

I attended one of ACRL's Intentional Teaching Immersion programs. My Information Science degree from the 90's did not have any courses on teaching. The program introduced us to many different teaching theories and encouraged us to develop a personal philosophy of teaching and apply it to our daily teaching practice. Through this class I discovered Parker Palmer. His writings and teaching philosophy resonated with me and taught me to be more reflective in my teaching.

—Candace Vance, Murray State University

I started out as a K-12 school librarian, so I came from a more teaching-focused background than I might have if I'd pursued an MLIS alone. After I became an academic librarian, I was still heavily focused on teaching and wanted to know how the learning/teaching theories I'd practiced with younger students would apply to the college-aged population.

—Anna Mary Williford, University of Montevallo

I was a reluctant teaching assistant in a political science Ph.D. program—completely absorbed by my own insecurity in the classroom. A library school course on information literacy instruction introduced me to the idea of student-centered teaching, to theories of power in the classroom, how people learn (and how they don't), and so forth. I still rely on the scholarship of teaching and learning to keep my focus on the students and away from any anxieties I may feel.

—Helen McManus, George Mason University

In your lesson planning, did you find the Framework or did the Framework find you?

Hide...

I really struggled with the Framework when it was first unveiled and I didn't want anything to do with it honestly. It seemed very nebulous and I couldn't get a good grip on what the concepts were about and how to apply them to my teaching. I'm fortunate to have an amazing colleague who really embraced the Framework and helped me to finally see the connections between the concepts and information literacy. It's natural now to match concepts to my lesson plans and it has strengthened how I teach and the activities I develop to teach.

—Mary Oberlies, University of Oregon

As a science faculty member, the Framework definitely found me, via my library liaison Nora Belzowski. She helped me to use the Framework to teach general education students the importance of scientific literacy.

—Kristi Bugajski, Valparaiso University

I was really trepidatious about the Framework, at first, and started exploring it because I was dubious, because I work with the sciences and was afraid people would perceive it as theory-driven and irrelevant. Instead I found it resonated really well with a lot of scientists, and lead to really engaging and delightful conversation that let us go beyond "find 3 peer reviewed articles" into the whys and how comes.

—Rebecca Kuglitsch, University of Colorado

I love the Framework and found that the threshold concepts mostly complemented and elucidated what I was already doing as an information literacy teacher and researcher. I found this to be particularly true in how I was teaching evaluation of sources, constructing arguments, and avoiding bias.

—Sharon Radcliff, California State University, East Bay

The Framework found me. I had long felt the mechanistic approach to information literacy was far too limiting. The Framework can help us get our students towards the big picture: how to ask questions and pursue inquiry.

—Yvonne Meulemans, California State University, San Marcos

Not only do I feel as though the Framework found me, but more importantly, I feel as though it found our students. The Framework validated a teaching style that places students at the center of learning, encourages active learning, and moves away from point-and-click instruction.

—Maoria Kirker, George Mason University

And Seek!

I am new to librarianship, as I worked as a law professor for the past ten years, so the Framework was one of the first things I learned as I began lesson planning for copyright outreach. I find the concepts in the Framework to be flexible, user-friendly, and adaptable. I have really appreciated utilizing the Framework as a basis for my instructional outreach.

—Sara Benson, University of Illinois

While I liked the old ACRL IL Standards' focus on the student's progression through the chaotic endeavor of research, I'm more taken by the Frameworks' shift in focus to teaching our students about the very nature of information and the process by which it is created, codified, used, and transferred. It urges a deeper understanding of what we call knowledge and what it means to "know" something in our current epistemological landscape.

—Victoria Elmwood, Loyola University of New Orleans

I think the Framework was a long time coming. It juxtaposes important aspects of learning theory with information literacy skills in an adaptable rather than prescriptive manner.

—Kelli Trei, University of Illinois at Urbana Champaign

I have only been a librarian for a few years, so I learned about the Framework as I learned about librarianship. The concepts in the frames feel very natural to me but I do not always feel as though I have instructional activities available to me that were designed with the frames in mind.

—Maglen Epstein, St. Olaf College

Around the same time that the Framework was being unveiled, the teaching faculty at my institution were adopting a new focus on critical thinking in the classroom. This initiative dovetailed so well with what the Framework was advocating that it seemed like the perfect time to start incorporating the Framework (with its emphasis on critical thinking) into our information literacy curriculum. The teaching faculty were able to get on board with it quickly because it resonated with what they were trying to accomplish in the classroom as well.

—Anna Mary Williford, University of Montevallo

The Framework came right on time when I started designing my lessons. When I found the Framework, I took to it immediately and began applying the frames to my instruction. I found that the threshold concepts gave me the language to communicate what I wanted my students to remember in five years from my lessons.

—Charissa Jefferson, California State University, Northridge

We learn from ourselves as much as we learn from others…

I try to pull as much information as possible from my mistakes to continue to hone my instruction skills.

—Kelli Trei, University of Illinois at Urbana Champaign

Every teaching opportunity is a chance to try out a new approach, a new discussion question, a new example, or a new activity. Great teachers constantly seek to improve their practice.

—Maglen Epstein, St. Olaf College

I always find inspiration from watching what other teachers are doing and by interacting with the students.

—Sharon Radcliff, California State University, East Bay

Learning/teaching theory doesn't tell you how to teach. It helps you understand how people learn, feel, and know. It enables you to imagine the perspectives of your students so that our work can be even more valuable to them and our community.

—Yvonne Nalani Meulemans, California State University, San Marcos

I find that my students learn as much from each other as they do from me (if not more!) so I have tried to put them in the driver's seat whenever possible. They have a lot to teach each other (and me!) and it is good for them to see each other struggling through tough concepts, so that they know it is a natural part of the learning process.

—Anna Mary Williford, University of Montevallo

You can learn a lot from your students, if you want to.

—Anne Leonard, New York City College of Technology

I had a lightbulb moment this past semester after trying to teach a class one way for several semesters. I felt frustrated when the students rejected the resources I was telling them were useful. They were all athletic students, confident, and used to being on the field. I realized I could use this to my advantage. I challenged them in a friendly way to find a better resource if they could, asked them how they would approach a search, and how they would evaluate the source they discovered. I've never had so many students from that class follow up with me after my visit. I created a team! It wasn't until that moment that I realized how much students want to be their own teachers. Social constructivism works!

—Janna Mattson, George Mason University

So, what's your best teaching story?

INDEX

B

C

D

F

J

K

L

M

N

Q

T